COLLECTS AND PRAYERS

FOR USE IN CHURCH

Collects and Prayers

FOR USE IN CHURCH

AUTHORIZED BY

THE UNITED LUTHERAN CHURCH
IN AMERICA

PREPARED BY

THE COMMON SERVICE BOOK COMMITTEE

PHILADELPHIA : PENNSYLVANIA

THE BOARD OF PUBLICATION OF
THE UNITED LUTHERAN CHURCH IN AMERICA

Copyright, 1935, by
THE BOARD OF PUBLICATION OF
THE UNITED LUTHERAN CHURCH IN AMERICA

MADE IN THE UNITED STATES OF AMERICA

FOREWORD

B ROADENING activities of life, within and without the Church, have made themselves felt in the devotional life of the Church in repeated requests for prayers and collects additional to those found in *The Common Service Book*.

Some years since the Common Service Book Committee undertook to meet this desire by appointing a sub-committee to plan a book of collects and prayers, outline in detail its scope and possible rubrics, and gather or provide the material. From time to time the results of the sub-committee's work were presented to the entire committee for study and criticism, and gradually the undertaking assumed such shape that a definite report of the proposed book could be made to The United Lutheran Church in America. In 1932 this body authorized its publication.

The Liturgy itself, with its invariable texts and its varying propers for Sundays, festivals, and other days, reflects the universal, unchanging needs of mankind, and brings these before the Throne of Grace in constant and manifold petition. There are many occasions, however, and many necessities of general import which properly call for special petitions in the assemblies of the faithful.

Christian people are interested not only in the work of the Church as such: they are deeply concerned also about the welfare of the community and the nation, and the well-being of all sorts and conditions of men. The common prayer of God's people, at particular times, may well reflect these hopes and desires in definite petitions inserted in the

General Prayer, in the use of specific collects and prayers at Matins and Vespers, in the devotional services of particular groups or organizations, or in family worship. The minister, also, has frequent occasion in his pastoral ministrations to offer prayer for specific necessities or for special gifts and graces.

It is not possible to cover all conditions, to foresee all emergencies, or to supply material which may be possible of use under all circumstances. The effort has been made, however, to provide prayers of specific intention and of liturgical dignity and propriety, which may be suggestively helpful even though modifications may need to be made in actual use.

Much of the published prayer literature of the Church has been studied in preparing this collection. Selections have been made from early Greek liturgies, from mediæval Mozarabic and Roman sources, from Anglican and Lutheran liturgies of the Reformation period, from the writings of the reformers, and from prayers by modern English, Scotch and American authors. In addition, a large number of the collects and prayers have been written by the editors, or secured by them from others, for this collection. The editors are responsible for the translations from the German and for the greater number of translations from the Latin. Care has been taken to preserve, as far as possible, the thought and spirit of the originals, but a freer translation has been necessary at times in order to adapt a useful ancient prayer to modern life.

It is hoped that the additional general prayers for the seasons of the Church Year will prove serviceable. The genius of the Lutheran Liturgy calls for a prayer of universal scope in The Service, and its proper use is directed by rubric. In this prayer the individual congregation unites with the whole Church in petitions for the good estate of the Church, the state, the home and family, education, morality, and other features of the commonweal, and in intercessions for the temporal and spiritual welfare of mankind. In this the Church, as the universal priesthood of believers, rises above purely personal and local considerations, and invokes the divine blessing upon all men, and upon every rightful institution and endeavor. This essential breadth of sympathy and petition should be preserved as one of the finest and most characteristic elements of the Church Service. The form which this general prayer shall take, however, may properly change from time to time.

Liturgical prayer, like the finest hymnody and music of the Church, constitutes a rich and constantly growing literature, to which the Church of every land and time makes contributions corresponding to its deeply felt needs and expressive of its special character and culture. It is the hope of the committee which has compiled and composed these prayers, that they may serve the Church in this our day, and aid it in its assemblies of worship in offering a sacrifice which shall be pure and acceptable.

———

It is a pleasure to record the gracious permission of writers, editors, and publishers who have granted us the privilege of using original or already published prayers. To these all we express sincere thanks. Acknowledgment is made in the bibliographical *Index of Sources*. It is our desire to give full credit to writer or publisher in every case possible. If this has not been done, or has not been done correctly, it is not because of lack of effort to locate and identify the prayer definitely. In any such case reported to the editors, due recognition will be accorded in any future printing of the collection.

As to the original collects and prayers in this book, permission to quote or print therefrom will be granted gladly and freely upon written application for the use of specific material; but no use of original material should be made until written permission has been granted.

The Common Service Book Committee as constituted during the years 1930-1932, 1932-1934

Luther D. Reed, *Chairman*
Harvey D. Hoover, *Secretary*

Robert D. Clare
Emil E. Fischer
William E. Fischer
Henry E. Jacobs
Edwin F. Keever
John F. Krueger
John C. Mattes
J. F. Ohl

Henry J. Pflum, Jr.
Gomer C. Rees
George R. Seltzer
Carl R. Simon
R. Morris Smith
August Steimle
M. L. Stirewalt
Paul Zeller Strodach

Calvin P. Swank

Sub-committee on book of Collects and Prayers

Emil E. Fischer
Luther D. Reed
Paul Zeller Strodach

CONTENTS

The Church

THE CHURCH

1—*For the Church Militant*

O GOD of unchangeable power and eternal light, look favorably on Thy whole Church, that wonderful and sacred mystery; and, by the tranquil operation of Thy perpetual providence, carry out the work of man's salvation; and let the whole world feel and see that things which were cast down are being raised up, that those things which had grown old are being made new, and that all things are returning to perfection, through Him from Whom they took their origin, even Jesus Christ our Lord. *Amen.*

2—*For the Church Militant*

O LORD JESUS CHRIST, Whom the glorious company of the Apostles and the noble army of Martyrs confessed with word and life: Make the Church, of which Thou art the Corner-Stone and which is built upon the foundation of Thine Apostles and Prophets, to keep the common confession clear and steadfast, ringing forth with the voice of holy faith and purest devotion; that fearlessly she may witness for Thee; teach the Word she hath from Thee; and stand forth boldly in the face of all the world to glorify Thee, Who with the Father and the Holy Ghost art God, blessed now and evermore. *Amen.*

3—*For the Church Militant*

O LORD GOD, Who dwellest on high yet delightest to have Thy habitation in the hearts of men; Who hast built Thy Church as a city upon a hill, and laid the foundations of it upon the Apostles and Prophets, Jesus Christ Himself being the chief Corner-Stone: Make us to be a spiritual building fit for the indwelling of Thy Holy Spirit, grounding us in faith, building us up in hope, and perfecting us in charity, that we, joined in the union of the Church Militant on earth, may enter into Thy Church Triumphant in heaven; through Jesus Christ, our Lord. *Amen.*

4—*For the Church Militant*

GRACIOUS FATHER, we humbly beseech Thee for Thy whole Church throughout the world. Fill it with all truth, and in all truth with all peace. Where it is corrupt, purify it; where it is in error, direct it; where it is superstitious, cleanse it; where anything is amiss, reform it; where it is right, strengthen and confirm it; where it is in want, furnish it; where it is divided and rent asunder, heal the breaches thereof, O Thou Holy One of Israel; through Jesus Christ, our Lord. *Amen.*

5—*For the Church Militant*

O LORD JESUS CHRIST, Whose train filled the Temple: Fill, we entreat Thee, with Thy life-giving Presence Thy living temple, the Church; her length, breadth, depth, height, her courts and outer courts. Make her every member a willing temple of the Holy Ghost. Bid her enlarge the place of her tent, that the fullness of the Gentiles may press in. Clothe her with Thy righteousness, adorn her with Thy graces, support her by Thy love of her and her love of Thee, crown her with Thy glory; Who livest and reignest with the Father and the Holy Ghost, One God, world without end. *Amen.*

6—*For the Church Militant*

O LORD JESUS CHRIST, Who art ever present with Thy Household in time; Who wilt consummate what Thou hast founded here in glory: Keep, we beseech Thee, Thy Church ever true to Thy divine will and purpose and cleanse her of every worldly and human taint; so that she may proclaim Thy entrusted Gospel boldly, fight sin and wrong unwaveringly, bear every burden courageously and endure every searching test steadfastly; that with **radiant** faith and love she may persevere in every worldly struggle and by Thy grace ever be victorious; Who with the Father and the Holy Ghost, livest and reignest, One God, world without end. *Amen.*

7—*For the Church Triumphant*

O GOD, before Whose face the generations rise and pass away, the Strength of those who labor and suffer, and the Repose of the holy and blessed dead: We rejoice in the Communion of Thy Saints. We remember all who have faithfully lived; all who have peacefully died, and especially those most dear to us (*who have entered into rest with Thee*). Lift us into light and love; and give us at last our portion with those who have trusted in Thee and striven in all things to do Thy holy will. And unto Thy Name, with the Church on earth and the Church in heaven, we ascribe all honor and glory, world without end. *Amen.*

8—*In Commemoration of the Faithful Departed*

ALMIGHTY GOD, with Whom do live the spirits of just men made perfect: We humbly commend the soul of this (*these*) Thy servant(*s*) into Thy hands, as into the hands of a faithful Creator and most merciful Saviour, most humbly beseeching Thee, that *he* may be precious in Thy sight. Wash *him*, we pray Thee, in the blood of that immaculate Lamb, Who was slain to take away the sin of the world; that *he* may be presented pure and without spot before Thee, to dwell for ever in the region of light, where is no weeping, sorrow, or heaviness, but sure consolation, eternal peace, and never ending joy; through Jesus Christ, our Lord. *Amen.*

9—*In Commemoration of the Faithful Departed*

O ALMIGHTY GOD, the God of the spirits of all flesh, Who by a voice from heaven didst proclaim, Blessed are the dead who die in the Lord: Multiply, we beseech

Thee, to those who rest in Jesus, the manifold blessings of Thy love, that the good work which Thou didst begin in them may be perfected unto the day of Jesus Christ. And of Thy mercy, O Heavenly Father, vouchsafe that we, who now serve Thee here on earth, may at the last, together with them, be found meet to be partakers of the inheritance of the saints in light; for the sake of the Same Thy Son, Jesus Christ, our Lord and Saviour. *Amen.*

10—*In Commemoration of the Faithful Departed*

O LORD GOD, the Light of the faithful, the Strength of those who labor, and the Repose of the blessed dead: We bless Thee for all Thy saints who have witnessed in their lives a good confession, and especially for those dear unto us who have fallen asleep in Jesus. Grant us grace, O Lord, so to follow their good example, that we may be one with them in spirit, and finally be partakers with them in Thy eternal rest; through Jesus Christ, our Lord. *Amen.*

11—*For the Consummation* (*For Use at Holy Communion*)

WE give thanks, our Father, for the life and the knowledge which Thou hast made known unto us through Jesus, Thy Servant; to Thee be the glory unto the ages. As this broken bread was scattered over the hills, and having been gathered became one, so may Thy Church be gathered from the ends of the earth into Thy Kingdom; for Thine is the glory and the power, through Jesus Christ, unto the ages. *Amen.*

12—*For the Consummation*

O LORD JESUS CHRIST, the First-fruits of them that slept: For those who die, we pray Thee, let death be sleep in Thee, and awaking be after Thy likeness: for those who shall be alive at Thy coming, we pray Thee, let Thine appearing be salvation, and Thy Word, Well done! Thou, Who with the Father and the Holy Ghost, art God, blessed now and evermore. *Amen.*

13—*World-wide Mission of the Church*

O GOD, our Heavenly Father, Who didst manifest Thy love by sending Thy Only-begotten Son into the world that all might live through Him: Pour Thy Spirit upon Thy Church that it may fulfil His command to preach the Gospel to every creature; send forth, we beseech Thee, laborers into Thy harvest; defend them in all dangers and temptations; and hasten the time when the fullness of the Gentiles shall be gathered in, and all Israel shall be saved; through Jesus Christ, our Lord. *Amen.*

14—*World-wide Mission of the Church*

O FATHER, we thank Thee for the Church which Thou hast raised up in many parts of the earth, and we pray for all those whom Thou hast called into it; guide them through perplexities; defend them amid oppression and hatred; strengthen and uphold those who face persecution for Christ's sake, and evermore enrich them with the gifts of Thy Spirit; through the Same Jesus Christ, our Lord. *Amen.*

15—*The Church and the Present Opportunity*

O LORD JESUS CHRIST, Who, in this our day, dost place before Thy Church a mighty opportunity for witnessing and service: Awaken us and all who call Thee Lord and Master to our holy privilege of laboring for Thee, and strengthen us to the accomplishing of Thy will, so that through the activities of Thy Body, the Church, the Gospel of redeeming love may be made known to the healing of the souls and lives of men; Thou, Who livest and reignest with the Father in the unity of the Holy Ghost, One God, world without end. *Amen.*

16—*The Church and the Restless World*

ALMIGHTY FATHER, Who hast so formed man for Thyself that his heart is restless till it finds rest in Thee: By the ministry of Thy Church and the lives of those who humbly love and follow Thee daily, convince the world that

Thou art the sure Refuge of all who are weary and distressed in mind and life, the safe Harbor to all who are restlessly seeking certainty and peace of heart, and the eternal Salvation of every burdened soul; so that coming to Thee they may find and possess that peace which Thou givest in Thy Son, our Saviour, Jesus Christ. *Amen.*

17—*The Church and the Community*

O GOD, Who through the gift of Thy Holy Spirit hast established the Church in this community: Grant unto all who have been converted unto Thee such a knowledge of Thy will and trust in Thy grace that they may truly exemplify the life that they profess, and by their good works enable men to glorify Thee, the only true God; through Jesus Christ, our Lord. *Amen.*

18—*The Church and the Community*

LORD JESUS CHRIST, Who dost send Thy Spirit to convict the world of sin, of righteousness and of judgment: Enable Thy Church by Thy Holy Spirit to set Thee before men in word and deed, so that the power of Thy Presence may be felt throughout our community, calling men away from every evil work to the fellowship of Thy glorious Gospel, and winning them to a life of blessed service with Thee in Thine everlasting Kingdom, Who livest and reignest with the Father and the Holy Ghost, One God, world without end. *Amen.*

19—*The Church and the Social Order*

O GOD, Whose Son, our Master, gave Himself unto Thee in all things, and for Thee unto all men, in order to reveal Thy will and love: Grant us grace and strength to live unto Thee and, following His blessed example, to love and serve others. Give us His vision that we may see life with sympathetic appreciation of its struggles and failures, its sin and needs. Give us His heart of love that we may not hesitate to work for the common good of our fellowmen.

Give us the blessed power of His Word, that we may speak with conviction and assurance, with healing comfort and love, to those whom we meet in the crowded ways of life, in home and shop, in school and church, and to those sitting in darkness and in the shadow of death. Give us His sympathy and comradeship that we may place ourselves beneath the burdens of others and sharing with them the strength which alone cometh from Thee, may we together with them endure and not lose heart. Give us His peace which is the benediction to hearts fast set in Thee and to life and service consecrated to Thee; through Jesus Christ, our Lord. *Amen.*

20—*The Church and Righteous Citizenship*

ALMIGHTY GOD, Who art the Ruler of the whole earth, and from Whom cometh all rule and authority among the peoples; make all who dwell in this our country mindful of Thy favor in granting us this goodly land as our heritage. Bless, we pray Thee, those whom the citizens of this country by their choice, have entrusted with the powers of government. Endue the people with the spirit of respect and willing obedience for wholesome law, and cause them to aid our chief executives, our judges and magistrates, in maintaining peace and righteousness throughout our borders. Enable us as a people brought hither out of many kindreds and tongues and knit together now as one nation, so to love and fear Thee, the God and Father of all mankind, that we may ever strive for that obedience to Thy holy law, which shall make us a nation acceptable unto Thee, and a people among whom Thy glory may ever dwell; through Jesus Christ, Thy Son, our Lord. *Amen.*

21—*For Church Unity*

O GOD, the Father of our Lord Jesus Christ, our only Saviour, the Prince of Peace: Give us grace seriously to lay to heart the great dangers we are in by our unhappy divisions; take away from us all hatred and prejudice, and whatsoever else may hinder us from godly union and concord; that as there is but one body, and one Spirit, and one hope of our calling, one Lord, one faith, one baptism, one God and Father of us all, so we may henceforth be all of one heart, and of one soul, united in one holy bond of truth and peace, of faith and charity, and may with one mind and one mouth glorify Thee; through Jesus Christ, our Lord. *Amen.*

22—*For Church Unity*

O GOD, our Father, Good beyond all that is good, Fair beyond all that is fair, in Whom is calmness and peace: Do Thou make up the dissensions which divide us from each other, and bring us back into a unity of love, which may bear some likeness to Thy sublime nature; grant that we may be spiritually one, as well in ourselves as in each other, through that peace of Thine which maketh all things peaceful, and through the grace, mercy, and tenderness of Thy Son, Jesus Christ, our Lord. *Amen.*

23—*For the Church in Our Land*

O LORD GOD, the Father of our Lord Jesus Christ, we thank Thee that Thou hast called us to the fellowship of grace, bound us together in the bonds of love and brotherhood in the Church established by Thy dear Son, and united our congregations and synods in a larger and effective union for service: Bless, we pray Thee, the Church, its officers and organizations, its ministers and people; grant that all may be one in Thee, and walk worthy of the Lord unto all pleasing, being fruitful in every good work and endeavoring to keep the unity of the Spirit in the bond of peace; through Jesus Christ, our Lord. *Amen.*

24—*For the Church in Our Land*

O SPIRIT Holy and Gracious, Who dost call, gather, enlighten and sanctify the whole Christian Church on earth, and preserve it in union with Jesus Christ in the true faith: Bless the Church, we pray Thee, with Thine especial guidance and grace; grant to all of us, its members, unity of brotherhood in Thee; faith unswerving; love unfailing; hope unending; fervor of sacrifice; zeal of service; consecration to the divine will; that by the healthful spirit of Thy grace, we may unitedly serve in the upbuilding and furtherance of the Kingdom of God and of our Lord Jesus Christ, Thou, Who livest and reignest with the Father and the Son, ever One God, world without end. *Amen.*

25—*For the Ministry*

O LORD, we beseech Thee to raise up for the work of the Ministry faithful and able men, who shall count it all joy to spend and be spent for the sake of Thy dear Son, and for the souls for whom He shed His most precious Blood upon the Cross; and fit them, we pray Thee, for their holy office by Thy bountiful grace and heavenly benediction; through the Same Jesus Christ, our Lord. *Amen.*

26—*For the Ministry*

O GOD, Whose ways are all mercy and truth: Carry on Thy gracious work, and bestow by Thy favor what human frailty cannot attain, that they who preach the Word and attend upon the heavenly mysteries may be grounded in perfect faith and shine forth by the purity of their lives; through Jesus Christ, our Lord. *Amen.*

27—*For the Ministry*

INCLINE the ears of Thy compassion, O most merciful God, to our prayers, which we offer to Thee for our pastors, that, their hearts being enlightened by the grace of Thy Holy Spirit and their lives sanctified by Thy truth, they may adorn the Gospel of our Lord Jesus Christ by their life and conversation, and be meet to minister before Thee in Thy Church on earth and to be partakers of eternal joy in Thy heavenly Kingdom; through the Same Jesus Christ, our Lord. *Amen.*

28—*For the Ministry*

O ALMIGHTY, Everlasting God, Who dost call men for the work of the Ministry, for the perfecting of the saints, for the edifying of the Body of Christ, and dost commit unto them Thy heavenly treasures that they may sow unto us spiritual things: As Thou hast instructed us in Thy holy Word, we remember before Thee this day all those who have the rule over us, the men who speak unto us Thy Word. We humbly thank Thee for their faithful witness; their loyal faith; their good examples; their devotion and unselfishness; and we pray that Thou wilt bless them with all grace so to serve Thee, and us with all grace so to receive and learn and to follow Thee, that we all may come, in the unity of the faith and of the knowledge of Thy Son, unto a perfect manhood, unto the measure of the stature of the fullness of Christ, our Lord. *Amen.*

29—*For Those about to be Ordained to the Holy Ministry*

O LORD, our God, Who by Thine own Presence dost shed the abundance of Thy Holy Spirit on those who are set apart to become ministers and to serve Thee: Keep Thy servants, who are about to be ordained to the office of the holy ministry; grant that they may hold the mystery of the faith in a pure conscience with all virtue; vouchsafe them Thy grace; enable them to minister according to Thy good pleasure; and fill them by the power of Thy Holy and Life-giving Spirit with all faith, and love, and power, and sanctification, for Thou art our God, and to Thee we render glory, through Jesus Christ, Thy Son, our Lord. *Amen.*

30—*For Deaconess' Work and the Ministry of Women*

O LORD, our Saviour Jesus Christ, Who in the days of Thy earthly ministry didst accept the service of godly women and the devotion of one who anointed Thy head and feet: Call Thou to the service of the Church in her ministry of mercy, many faithful women; and as they go forth sustain and direct them in their work, and grant unto them the blessing which Thou hast promised to those who give a cup of cold water to the least of Thy brethren; Who livest and reignest with the Father and the Holy Ghost, One God, world without end. *Amen.*

31—*For Such as Administer the Affairs of the Church*

O LORD, without Whom our labor is but lost, and in Whom our weakness is made strength: Be present to bless all the works of Thy Church which are undertaken according to Thy will. Grant that all whom Thou dost choose to work for Thee may labor in union with Thy holy purposes and in living unity with Thy dear Son; that by the power of Thy Holy Spirit they may accomplish far more than they ever know, and work not for results but singly for the love of Thee; through the Same Thy Son, Jesus Christ, our Lord. *Amen.*

32—*For the Church Council*

LORD GOD, Heavenly Father, Who according to Thy gracious will, hast established within Thy Church on earth, besides the ministry of the Word, other offices for the ministration of Thy manifold gifts of grace: We thank Thee, that, in this place, Thou hast provided men of honest report, ready to serve this congregation for Thy sake; and we humbly pray Thee to enrich them abundantly with Thy Holy Spirit, that they may have wisdom and strength for the service unto which Thou hast called them; through Jesus Christ, our Lord. *Amen.*

33—*For a Meeting of the Church Council*

ALMIGHTY and Eternal God, the Giver of grace and strength: We beseech Thee to bestow Thy blessing upon us, who have been placed in positions of trust in Thy holy Church. Give us a clear sense of our duty and lead us to a faithful discharge of the same. Grant us gentleness, forbearance, a right judgment and personal consecration, that by precept and example, as well as by our official actions, the temporal and spiritual good of Thy Church may be enlarged. Especially direct us in our counsels by Thy gracious Spirit, so that all things may be done to the glory of Thy Name, and for the unity, peace, and prosperity of this parish. We ask this for the sake of Jesus Christ our Lord. *Amen.*

34—*For the Choir*

O GOD, in Whose Temple at Jerusalem were appointed singers and those skilled in instruments of music to set forth Thy praises: Be present, we beseech Thee, with us Thy servants, and grant that in this our service we may worship Thee in spirit and in truth, and at last be found meet to glorify Thy Name in Thy Temple which is on high; through Jesus Christ, our Lord. *Amen.*

35—*For the Choir*

O GOD, to Whom the cherubim and seraphim adoringly sing: Grant that as our voices are uplifted in this service to Thy praise, so we may continually sing and make melody in our hearts unto Thee; through Jesus Christ, our Lord. *Amen.*

36—*In the Choir Vestry (Before Service)*

O GOD, let Thy grace descend upon us and fill our hearts; that with true reverence we may magnify Thy holy Name; through Jesus Christ, our Lord. *Amen.*

37

O GOD, Who art ever present in Thy holy temple: Sanctify our hearts by Thy Spirit that we may render unto Thee worthy praise and laudable service; through Jesus Christ, our Lord. *Amen.*

38

O GOD, cleanse our hearts and purify our lips that with lowliness and reverence of mind we may worship Thee in spirit and in truth; through Jesus Christ, our Lord. *Amen.*

39—*In the Choir Vestry* (*After Service*)

GRANT, O LORD, that what we have sung with our lips we may believe in our hearts and practice in our lives; through Jesus Christ, our Lord. *Amen.*

40

DISMISS us now, O Lord, with Thy blessing, and accompany us ever with Thy grace, that we may henceforth live in peace, love, and holiness; through Jesus Christ, our Lord. *Amen.*

41

LET the words of our mouth and the meditations of our heart be acceptable in Thy sight, O Lord, our Strength and our Redeemer. *Amen.*

42—*For the Ministry of Music*

O GOD, Who by Thy servant David didst appoint for the Levites instruments of music of the Lord, to praise Thee, because Thy mercy endureth for ever: Graciously vouchsafe to accept this our sacrifice of prayer and praise, that we may sing our songs all the days of our life in the house of the Lord; and grant us so to do with the spirit and with the understanding also, that we may be counted among them who shall sing the new song before Thy throne; through Jesus Christ, our Lord. *Amen.*

43—*Catechumens*

LORD JESUS CHRIST, Who didst lay the hand of Thy blessing upon the little ones who came unto Thee, declaring that of such is the Kingdom of Heaven: We present before Thee in this our prayer these who are being instructed in Thy way; and beseech Thee give them knowledge and understanding in all that will make their lives a praise unto Thee, and add thereto the increase of piety, so that they may know Thee, truly fear Thee, fervently love

Thee, and ever keep Thy commandments; Who livest and reignest with the Father and the Holy Ghost, One God, world without end. *Amen.*

44—*For Those Who Have Been Confirmed*

O GOD, Whose Spirit multiplies and rules the whole body of the Church: Conserve in those who have dedicated themselves to Thy service, the grace of sanctification, which Thou alone dost impart; so that renewed in body and mind, they may serve Thee zealously in the unity of the faith; through Jesus Christ, our Lord. *Amen.*

45—*For Those Who Have Been Confirmed*

O LORD JESUS, Who hast promised that Thou wilt confess before Thy Father in heaven those who confess Thee before men: Grant to those who have sealed their faith before Thy altar, grace and strength ever to put away from them all things contrary to their profession and in humble and persevering faith to follow after all things pleasing to Thee, Who livest and reignest with the Father and the Holy Ghost, One God, world without end. *Amen.*

46—*For a Conference of Christian People*

O LORD JESUS CHRIST, Master of men, Whom to see is to love, and Whom to know is eternal life: in Thy life we see all things which we fain would be; therefore do Thou draw near to us now as we would come near to Thee. In these *days* (*hours*) of conference may the influence of Thy gracious Spirit be with us enabling us to surrender ourselves to Thy love and service. And when we go down from here may the vision not fade, and our loyalty not slacken. Abide with us. So shall we grow daily into the likeness of Thy Spirit. And to Thee, together with the Father and the Holy Spirit, One God, be all glory and praise, now and evermore. *Amen.*

47—*For a Conference of Christian People*

ALMIGHTY GOD, without Whom nothing is strong, nothing is holy: May our speaking and hearing at this time be to the increase of faith, hope, and love. May all that is untrue perish in the speaking, and all that is true be preserved for our use and Thy service; through Jesus Christ our Lord. *Amen.*

48—*For a Retreat or Quiet Day*

O LORD JESUS CHRIST, Who didst withdraw Thyself unto a mountain for prayer, and didst bring Thy Apostles apart from the multitude, that they might rest a while with Thee: Be graciously present, we beseech Thee, with us who are gathered together in Thy Name, and grant that we, profitably meditating in Thy Word and inspired thereby with a good will to serve Thee, may diligently fulfil the same. *Amen.*

49—*For a Retreat or Quiet Day*

O LORD JESUS CHRIST, Who didst say to Thy disciples, Come ye apart and rest a while: Grant, we beseech Thee, to Thy servants now gathered together, so to seek Thee, Whom our souls desire to love, that we may both find Thee and be found of Thee; and grant such love and such wisdom to accompany the words which shall be spoken in Thy Name, that they may not fall to the ground, but may be helpful in leading us onward to Thy perfect service; Who with the Father and the Holy Ghost, livest and reignest, One God, world without end. *Amen.*

The Parish

THE PARISH

50—*General*

ALMIGHTY and Everlasting God, Who dost govern all things in heaven and in earth: Mercifully hear our prayers, and grant to our parish all things needful to its spiritual and temporal welfare. Strengthen and confirm the faithful; visit and relieve the sick; comfort those who mourn; grant Thy peace to the aged; arouse the indifferent and careless; recover the fallen; forgive and receive the penitent; and remove all hindrances to the advancement of Thy truth, bringing us all to be of one mind within the fold of Thy holy Church, to the honor and glory of Thy ever-blessed Name; through Jesus Christ, our Lord. *Amen.*

51—*For a Parish without a Pastor*

O GOD, Who knowest the needs of Thy Church in every place: Look graciously at this time upon the people of this parish; and give to them a faithful pastor, who may serve before Thee in all diligence and lowliness of heart, and, by Thy blessing, bring many souls to the joys of Thine eternal Kingdom; through Jesus Christ, our Lord. *Amen.*

52—*At the Time of an Election of a Pastor*

O LORD JESUS CHRIST, Who art the Head of Thy Body, the Church, and the Shepherd and Bishop of souls: Be present, we pray Thee, with this congregation now assembled for the purpose of calling a pastor; strengthen all hearts and minds by the purifying and enlightening power of the Holy Spirit, so that, mindful only of the welfare of this congregation and of Thy holy Church, *these*

Thy servants (*we*) may be guided of Thee in *their* (*our*) decisions, and a godly and able pastor finally be chosen to minister to *them* (*us*) in all spiritual good, to the honor of Thy Name and the upbuilding of Thy Kingdom here among men; Who livest and reignest with the Father and the Holy Spirit, One God, world without end. *Amen.*

53—*For a Pastor Entering upon the Duties of a Parish*

ALMIGHTY and Eternal God, Who dost call men to be pastors of Thy people and ministers of Thy grace: We thank Thee that Thou hast called Thy servant to minister to this congregation and to serve before Thee in Thy sanctuary; vouchsafe to him as he now begins his ministry in this place, the direction, aid and counsel of Thy Holy Spirit; that he may serve Thee with a pure heart and holy life; preach Thy Word according to Thy loving purpose in Christ Jesus; humbly and devoutly administer Thy sacraments; and be found in all things acceptable to Thee as a good and faithful steward; through Jesus Christ, Thy Son our Lord. *Amen.*

FOR ORGANIZATIONS OF THE CONGREGATION OR PARISH

54—*For Men's Organizations*

O LORD JESUS CHRIST, Who hast committed the administration of Thy Church's business and service to the stewardship of men: Grant us ever to remember that the work which we are to do is eternal and the ends which we are to serve are wholly Thine; that Thine is the responsibility but ours is the obedience; so that we may yield our will to Thy direction and kindle our zeal by Thy example; and losing all thought of self, in humble consecration to Thy Kingdom's work, find the joy of faithful stewardship; Who with the Father and the Holy Ghost, livest and reignest, One God, world without end. *Amen.*

55—*For Men's Organizations*

O LORD JESUS, Who through Thy Apostle hast taught us that Thy Church is one brotherhood in Thee: Bless, we pray Thee, this union of the Men of the Church unto the service of the greater brotherhood; that through our fellowship with Thee and each other we may find grace to live and work for the upbuilding of Thy Kingdom; Who with the Father and the Holy Ghost, livest and reignest, One God, world without end. *Amen.*

56—*For Women's Organizations*

O LORD JESUS, loved and served by the devoted women in the Gospel, Friend of Mary and Martha: Graciously accept our ministry which we humbly consecrate to the service of Thy Kingdom; let Thy blessing attend it and make it ever fruitful that through it Thy Name may be glorified and many may be brought to know, and love, and follow Thee; enrich us with the joy of selfless devotion; direct and control our every purpose; strengthen our hands and hearts, that while we are busy in serving we still may ever possess the better part, blessed communion with Thee; Who with the Father and the Holy Ghost, livest and reignest, One God, world without end. *Amen.*

57—*For Women's Organizations*

GRANT us, O Father, we beseech Thee, through Jesus Christ our Advocate, the gift of Thy Holy Spirit, that quickened and led by Him we may both have grace to see and courage and fidelity to grasp our privileges and to perform our tasks in Thy Kingdom here; and as all our labor without Thee is but vain, be present with our society here and in all its branches, ever directing us into such fields of usefulness as will serve Thy will and granting us every gift needful to the accomplishment of this service; through the Same Thy Son, Jesus Christ, our Lord. *Amen.*

58—For Men and Women in the Organizations of the Church

O LORD GOD, Who dost rule in the hearts and lives of the faithful: Vouchsafe to us, Thy servants, a spirit of ready obedience to Thy Word and earnest devotion to the labors of Thy Church, that in our every action we may worthily serve Thee, our King; through Jesus Christ, our Lord. *Amen.*

59—For Young People's Organizations

O ALMIGHTY GOD, Whose years know no end, before Whom the generations rise and pass away, our gracious Father: Teach us to number our days now in our youth and apply our hearts unto eternal wisdom, that we may choose the way of life and ever follow after holiness of living, knowing that in all our thoughts, and words, and works we are building upon the foundation laid in Jesus Christ, Thy Son, to the end that we grow up unto Him into the full stature of manhood in Christ Jesus, Who liveth and reigneth with Thee and the Holy Ghost, One God, world without end. *Amen.*

60—For Young People's Organizations ·

ALMIGHTY GOD, Whose blessed Son didst take our nature upon Him, leaving us an example that we should follow His steps: Look graciously with Thy favor upon our youth, and make them to grow in wisdom and stature and in favor with Thee, their God. Give them grace to remember Thee now in the days of their youth, and to consecrate their strength to Thy service; preserve them from the sins which easily beset them, and deliver them out of all temptations; keep them pure in heart, upright in life, and diligent in the work to which they have been called. Looking unto Jesus, the author and finisher of their faith, may they go from strength to strength and at last, having finished their course and kept the faith, receive from Thee the crown of life that fadeth not away; through the Same Jesus Christ our Lord. *Amen.*

61—*General—For Any Organization*

LORD and Master, Who dost accept even the giving of a cup of cold water in Thy Name: We thank Thee for the opportunities of service, and beseech Thee to keep us faithful in doing the little things well and the common daily things gladly, that, each one of us being found faithful in his own calling, though poor we may make many rich, and having nothing we may at last possess all things; Who livest and reignest with the Father and the Holy Ghost, One God, world without end. *Amen.*

Divine Worship

DIVINE WORSHIP

62—*For the Spirit of True Worship*

O ALMIGHTY GOD, from Whom every good prayer cometh, and Who pourest out on all who desire it the Spirit of grace and supplication: Deliver us when we draw nigh to Thee from all coldness of heart and wanderings of mind, that with steadfast thoughts and kindled affections we may worship Thee in spirit and in truth; through Jesus Christ, our Lord. *Amen.*

63—*For the Spirit of True Worship*

O HEAVENLY FATHER, forasmuch as none can come to receive Thy holy Word except Thou draw them by Thy gracious inspiration: We beseech Thee to pour out Thy Holy Spirit upon those who worship today in Thy holy house of prayer, that their hearts may be inclined favorably to receive, steadfastly to retain, and obediently to perform, whatsoever shall be taught them in Thy Name; and that they may manifest in the dedication to Thee of their lives and substance, that thankfulness which they owe to Thee for Thy redeeming love; through Jesus Christ, our Lord. *Amen.*

64—*For Those Who Worship*

O GOD, Who dost call all men to Thee, and Who dost graciously receive all them that come: Vouchsafe Thy pardon to all those who here confess their sins; bestow the comfort of Thy Spirit on those who humbly and faithfully bring Thee their needs and sorrows; accept the praise and worship that are offered here; and grant that many may find Thee in this place, and finding Thee, be filled in soul and body with all things needful; and finally, with all Thine own, be united in that communion with Thee which is eternal in the heavens, where Thou livest and reignest, ever One God, world without end. *Amen.*

65—For Fruitful Hearing of the Word

ALMIGHTY and Everlasting God, Whose Word in the Holy Scriptures and in the ministrations of Thy house is implanted in our hearts, even as seed is sown in the ground: Grant us receptive minds, we pray Thee, good and honest hearts, free from selfishness and sin; so that by the quickening power of Thy Spirit we may become not hearers only, but doers of the Word; and, having the eyes of our understanding enlightened and the spirit of our mind renewed, be enabled to bring forth spiritual fruit in all goodness and righteousness and truth, proving what is acceptable unto Thee and serviceable unto our fellowmen; through Jesus Christ, Thy Son, our Lord. *Amen.*

66—For Fruitful Hearing of the Word

ALMIGHTY, Everlasting God, Lord, Heavenly Father, Whose Word is a lamp to our feet and a light on our way: Open and enlighten our minds that we may understand Thy Word purely, clearly and devoutly, and fashion our lives according to the same; through Jesus Christ, our Lord. *Amen.*

67—For Increase in the Knowledge of Christ

GRANT us, O Lord, an ever-growing, ever-deepening experience of the truth as it is in Christ Jesus. Grant that we may learn it, not only with our minds, but in our hearts. Grant that with lengthening years we may have increasing proof of it in our lives; and give us wisdom, that we may use it, as Jesus did, in the service of our fellowmen; through the Same Jesus Christ, our Lord. *Amen.*

68—For Increase in the Knowledge of God

O GOD, Who didst send Thy Son to live with men that, through Him, they might know Thee truly, love Thee purely, and worship Thee aright: Remove far from us all the wrong desires that cloud our vision when we look on Him; and bestow upon us the aid of Thy Holy Spirit, that knowing Christ, we may come to an ever truer knowledge of Thyself; through the Same, Thy Son, Jesus Christ, our Lord. *Amen.*

69—*Upon Entering Church*

O GOD, Whose Word is a light making bright my way to Thee: Open my ears to hear, my mind to understand, my heart and soul to receive, my life to show forth, Thy blessed Word borne to me this day; through Jesus Christ, our Lord. *Amen.*

70—*Upon Entering Church*

O LORD, open Thou my lips to praise Thy Name, for I would adore Thee in Thy Church, O Blessed God, Father, Son, and Holy Spirit, Who art worthy of all adoration and worship, blessing and praise, now and evermore. *Amen.*

71—*Upon Entering Church*

B LESS me, O God, with a reverent sense of Thy Presence, that in its glory, I may be still and adore Thee; through Jesus Christ, our Lord. *Amen.*

72—*Upon Entering Church (At a Time of Holy Communion)*

D IRECT and control us, O Lord, always and everywhere with heavenly light; that we may both discern with pure vision and share with worthy effect that mystery of which Thou hast willed us to partake; through Jesus Christ, our Lord. *Amen.*

73—*For Reverence in God's House*

O LORD, Who in Thy righteous zeal didst cast out the profaners of Thy Father's house: Enter, by Thy Spirit, into the temple of our hearts, and so cleanse us from all sinful thoughts and vain imaginations, that the sacrifice of our worship may be well-pleasing unto Thee, and we may reverence the place where Thine honor dwelleth; Who with the Father and the Holy Ghost, livest and reignest, One God, world without end. *Amen.*

74—*For Reverence for God's House*

O GOD, most High and most Holy; of Whom, and through Whom, and to Whom are all things; Whose glory no man can approach unto, yet Who hast deigned to tabernacle with men in an earthly house, where Thou hast welcome all who seek Thee: Fill us, we implore Thee, with most humble reverence of Thyself, and for all that belongs to Thy holy Name, Thy house, Thy worship, Thy Word, Thy sacraments. Pardon our unworthiness; enable us to present ourselves, our souls and bodies, a living sacrifice, holy and acceptable unto Thee. Let our praises and prayers, as the odor of sweet incense, come before Thee, so that we may rejoice in Thy Presence here; and learning in these Thy sacred courts ever to be more and more holy in heart and life, may we at the last be counted worthy to enter Thy temple above and to live in Thy Presence for evermore; through Jesus Christ, our Lord. *Amen.*

PRIVATE PRAYERS BEFORE HOLY COMMUNION

75—*Before Communion*

A LMIGHTY GOD, Everlasting Father, Who dost refresh us as we have need, and dost strengthen our faith with heavenly food, so that we go from strength to strength: Vouchsafe to us and to all who receive at Thy altar this day the holy sacrament of the Body and Blood of Thy dear Son, to approach this holy mystery with pure hearts, believing desire, and devout thanksgiving, that, comforted with Thy eternal love and goodness, we may be nourished and strengthened in faith, live in love and to the praise of Thy holy Name, and finally attain to Thy Presence in eternity; through the Same Jesus Christ, our Lord. *Amen.*

76—*Before Communion*

WE do not presume to come to this Thy table, O Merciful Lord, trusting in our own righteousness, but in Thy manifold and great mercies: We be not worthy so much as to gather up the crumbs under Thy table; but Thou art the same Lord Whose property is always to have mercy; grant us therefore, gracious Lord, so to eat the Flesh of Thy dear Son, and to drink His Blood in these holy mysteries, that we may continually dwell in Him and He in us, that our sinful bodies may be made clean by His Body, and our souls washed through His most precious Blood. *Amen.*

77—*Before Communion*

WE render Thee thanks, O Lord, our God, that Thou hast given us boldness to enter into the holiest, through the Blood of Jesus, by the new and living way which Thou hast consecrated through the veil of the flesh of Thy Christ; therefore, thus entering into the tabernacle of Thy glory and brought within the veil, we fall down before Thee in adoration and awe: but Thou, O Lord, send forth Thy grace and hallow our souls, bodies and spirits, so that with pure hearts we may offer to Thee our sacrifice of praise and thanksgiving; through the Same Jesus Christ, our Lord. *Amen.*

78—*Before Communion*

GLORY be to Thee, O Lord Jesus Christ! Welcome to my soul, Lord Jesus, with the precious food of Thy most holy Body, Which, with the consecrated bread, Thou now givest me to eat in Thy sacrament, as Thou gavest It for me in Thy bitter Death on the Cross for the forgiveness of my sins. May This bless me unto everlasting life. *Amen.*

79—*Before Communion*

GLORY be to Thee, O Lord Jesus Christ! Welcome to my soul, Lord Jesus, with the precious Drink of Thy most holy Blood, Which, with the consecrated wine, Thou givest me to drink in Thy sacrament, as Thou didst pour

It out on the Cross for the forgiveness of my sins. May This bless me unto everlasting life. *Amen.*

80—*Before Communion*

LORD, I am not worthy that Thou shouldest come unto me, but, as Thou hast promised, I beseech Thee, tabernacle with me, and my soul shall be healed. *Amen.*

81—*Before Communion*

BLESSED LORD JESUS, Who art ever inviting us to come unto Thee, and Who dost come so graciously even unto us Thine unworthy servants, in the holy sacrament of Thy Body and Blood:

ACCORDING to Thy Word we come to Thy altar, humbly but joyfully, to meet Thee; therefore, we beseech Thee, help us to prepare ourselves to receive Thee in adoring love and welcome; so that Thou wilt find in us a mansion fit for Thy indwelling.

GRANT US, we pray, true repentance for our many sins; unwavering faith in Thee, Who didst give Thyself on the Cross for us; the sure comfort of Thy forgiveness; the cleansing of our hearts of all that is wrong between us and our neighbor; and firm purpose to better our lives from day to day; so that having received Thee, we may live in constant and closest union with Thee, nevermore forgetting Thee, our precious guest, or driving Thee away by wilful selfishness, denial, or disloyalty; but rejoicing in Thy love, live to Thy praise; Who with the Father and the Holy Ghost, livest and reignest, One God, world without end. *Amen.*

PRIVATE PRAYERS AFTER HOLY COMMUNION

82—*After Communion*

GLORY be to Thee, my Lord and my God, for thus feeding me with Thy most blessed Body and Blood! Let this heavenly good impart new life and vigor to me, and to all who communicate with me, that our faith may increase daily, that we may become humble and contrite for our sins, may love Thee, serve Thee, delight in Thee, and praise Thee more fervently and constantly than we have ever done before; O Thou, Who with the Father and the Holy Ghost, livest and reignest, One God, world without end. *Amen.*

83—*After Communion*

O MERCIFUL FATHER, we render Thee thanks and praise that Thou hast vouchsafed to feed us, Thy unworthy servants, with the precious Body and Blood of Thy dear Son; and we pray, that by Thy grace, we may walk worthy of our holy calling and learn to adorn the doctrine of God our Saviour in all things; through the Same Jesus Christ, Thy Son, our Lord. *Amen.*

84—*After Communion*

GRANT, O Lord, that the ears which have heard the voice of Thy songs may be closed to the voice of clamor and dispute; that the eyes which have seen Thy great love may also behold Thy blessed hope; that the tongues which have united in the Sanctus may speak the truth; that the feet which have walked in Thy courts may walk in the region of light; and that the souls of all who have received Thy blessed sacrament may be restored in newness of life. Glory be to Thee for Thine unspeakable gift; Who with the Father and the Holy Ghost, livest and reignest, One God, world without end. *Amen.*

The Church Building

THE CHURCH BUILDING

85—*For the Builders of a Church*

O GOD, Who art the Shield and Defence of Thy people: Be ever at hand, we beseech Thee, to protect and succor all who labor in the building of this house; keep them in their work from all sin and profaneness, and shelter them from all accident and peril; that that which, under Thy mercy, hath now been begun, may by their labors be brought to a happy end; through Jesus Christ, our Lord. *Amen.*

86—*For the Builders of a Church*

O ETERNAL GOD, mighty in power, of infinite majesty, Whom the heaven of heavens cannot contain, much less the walls of temples made with hands; Who yet hast promised to be present wherever two or three are gathered together in Thy Name: Direct and bless, we pray Thee, our efforts to build this house for Thy worship and service, and grant us such success as may tend to Thy glory and the salvation of Thy people; through Jesus Christ, our Lord. *Amen.*

87—*Upon Completion of the Building of a Church*

L ORD GOD of our fathers, Who of old time hast accepted them that labored willingly upon the house of God, and hast filled men with Thy Spirit to devise skilful works in all manner of workmanship for the service of the sanctuary: We thank Thee that Thou hast enabled us to build this house to Thy praise, and we beseech Thee to accept the completed labors of our hands to Thy glory; and grant that in this holy and beautiful house we and our children may worship and serve Thee; through Jesus Christ, our Lord. *Amen.*

88—*For the Anniversary of the Dedication of a Church*

O GOD, Who year after year dost return to us the day of the dedication of this Thy holy temple, and ever dost bring us again into the presence of Thy holy mysteries: Hear the prayers of Thy people, and grant that whosoever shall enter this temple about to seek blessings may rejoice to have had his desires wholly fulfilled; through Jesus Christ, our Lord. *Amen.*

Missions

MISSIONS

89—*General*

ALMIGHTY GOD, Who by Thy Son Jesus Christ didst give commandment to the Apostles that they should go into all the world and preach the Gospel to every creature: Grant to us whom Thou hast called into Thy Church a ready will to obey Thy Word, and fill us with a hearty desire to make Thy way known upon earth, Thy saving health among all nations. Look with compassion upon the heathen that have not known Thee, and upon the multitudes that are scattered abroad as sheep having no shepherd. O heavenly Father, Lord of the harvest, have respect, we beseech Thee, to our prayers, and send forth laborers into Thy harvest. Fit and prepare them by Thy grace for the work of Thy ministry; give them the Spirit of power and of love and of a sound mind; strengthen them to endure hardness; and grant that Thy Holy Spirit may prosper their work, and that by their life and doctrine they may show forth Thy glory, and set forward the salvation of all men; through Jesus Christ, our Lord. *Amen.*

90—*For the Triumph of the Gospel*

O LORD JESUS CHRIST, by Whom came grace and truth, with Thy truth send forth Thy grace, we entreat Thee, throughout all the world, and hasten that day when the earth shall be full of the knowledge of the Lord, as the waters cover the sea. Impart true wisdom to those who as yet know Thee not, that they may behold, accept, love and cleave to Thee, their only Saviour; and preserve in the way of Thy truth such as now walk therein. *Amen.*

91—*Evangelistic Work*

INCREASE, O God, the faith and zeal of all Thy people, that they may more earnestly desire, and more diligently seek the salvation of their fellowmen through the message of Thy love in Jesus Christ, our Lord. Move Thy servants to preach Thy Word with power and grace, and multiply the number of those who labor in the Gospel, granting unto them a heart of love, sincerity of speech, and the manifold gifts of the Holy Ghost; that they may be able to lead men to forsake sin and to turn unto Thee. And so bless and favor all who labor for Thee in the seeking of souls that multitudes may be brought from the kingdom of evil into the Kingdom of Thy dear Son, our Saviour, Jesus Christ, our Lord. *Amen.*

92—*Inner Missions*

O LORD JESUS CHRIST, Who, in the days of Thy flesh, wast moved with compassion because of the bodily as well as the spiritual needs of men, and Who, as a true and faithful Shepherd, dost even now follow Thy lost sheep into the wilderness: Grant us grace, we beseech Thee, to have pity upon all whom Thou dost pity, and, after Thy holy example, to seek to bring deliverance from sin and all its evil fruits to all who suffer in body or soul; Who with the Father and the Holy Ghost livest and reignest, One God, world without end. *Amen.*

93—*City Missions*

O GOD, Almighty and Merciful, Who healest those that are broken in heart, and turnest the sadness of the sorrowful to joy: Let Thy fatherly goodness be upon all that Thou hast made; especially, we beseech Thee, to remember in pity such as are, at this time, destitute, homeless, or forgotten of their fellowmen. Bless the congregation of Thy poor. Uplift those who are cast down; befriend all innocent sufferers; and sanctify to them the endurance of their wrongs. Cheer with hope all discouraged and unhappy people, and by Thy heavenly grace preserve from falling those whose destitution tempteth them to sin. Though they be troubled on every side, suffer them not to be distressed; though they be perplexed, save them from despair. Grant this, O Lord, for the love of Him, Who for our sakes became poor, even Thy Son, Jesus Christ, our Saviour. *Amen.*

94—*Workers in City Missions*

GRACIOUS GOD and Father, Who willest not that any should perish, but that all men should be saved and come to the knowledge of the truth: Bless and encourage all workers who are ministering to the poor, the destitute, the wanderers and outcasts in our great cities. Give them patience in dealing with the vicious and forsaken, and persistence in seeking all who have gone astray; that as Thy Son, our blessed Lord, came to seek and to save the lost, so they, in His Name, may ever seek to bring them back to Thee; through the Same, Thy Son, Jesus Christ, our Lord. *Amen.*

95—*Home Missions*

O GOD, Who hast commanded Thy faithful people not to forsake the assembling of themselves together; we beseech Thee for all in our own land who are scattered abroad as sheep without a shepherd. Mercifully send unto them godly and faithful missionaries and pastors; and help us to speed them on their way, that Thy Word may everywhere be preached, and famished souls be fed with the bread of life to the glory of Thy holy Name; through the Same, Jesus Christ, our Lord. *Amen.*

96—*Home Missions*

O LORD JESUS CHRIST, Who didst send forth Thy disciples to declare the tidings of Thy coming: We beseech Thee to be present in Thy power with all the missions of Thy Church in this our land and enable Thy servants to gather the multitudes into Thy fold. Especially do we beseech Thee to show forth Thy compassion to the helpless; to enlighten the ignorant; to succor those in peril; and at the last to bring all Thy children home to Thyself; Who livest and reignest with the Father and the Holy Ghost, One God, world without end. *Amen.*

97—*Foreign Missions*

O GOD, Who hast made of one blood all nations of men for to dwell on the face of the whole earth, and didst send Thy blessed Son to preach peace to them that are far-off and to them that are nigh: Grant that all men everywhere may seek after Thee and find Thee; bring the nations into Thy fold, and pour out Thy Spirit upon all flesh, and hasten Thy Kingdom; through the Same, Thy Son, Jesus Christ, our Lord. *Amen.*

98—*Foreign Missions*

A LMIGHTY GOD, Who hast promised to give Thy Son the heathen for His inheritance, and the uttermost parts of the earth for His possession: Bless, we beseech Thee, the missionary work of Thy holy Church in all parts of the world. Have pity upon all who are still calling upon false gods; enlighten them by Thy Spirit through the Gospel of Thy Son, that they may turn to Thee, the living God, Who wouldest have all men to be saved and to come to the knowledge of the truth. Raise up from among them, we pray Thee, prophets and teachers, full of wisdom and of the Holy Ghost; and out of many nations and people and kindreds and tongues, gather the congregation of Thy saints; through the Same Jesus Christ, Thy Son, our Lord. *Amen.*

99—*Foreign Missions*

O GOD, Who didst send the Holy Spirit to enkindle the zeal of Christ's followers: Magnify the power of the Gospel in our hearts, that it may be to us the sacred truth for the blessing of mankind. Enable Thy Church to spread the good news of salvation, so that all nations may hear it in their own tongue, and welcome it into their own life. Protect, encourage, and bless all missionaries of the Cross; and prosper their word and work; so that Jesus, being lifted up, may draw all men unto Him, and the kingdoms of the world may become the Kingdom of our Lord and of His Christ. *Amen.*

100—*Educational Missions*

O GOD, Who art the Goal of all knowledge and the Source of all truth, Who dost lead mankind towards Thyself along the paths of discovery and learning, direct with Thy wise Spirit the work of education in every land. Especially do we pray for those who have been called to teach in foreign lands; give them insight into the needs of those whom they instruct and enable them to understand their life and ways that they may minister to them in wisdom and grace. Give them that beauty of life without which knowledge is vain, and enable them to bring those whom they teach to the feet of the Master, to receive His gift of eternal life; through the Same, Jesus Christ, our Lord. *Amen.*

See also No. 125.

101—*For Missionaries*

O GOD, our Saviour, Who willest that all men should be saved and come to the knowledge of the truth: Prosper, we pray Thee, our brethren who labor in distant lands, (*especially those for whom our prayers are desired*). Protect them in all perils; support them in loneliness and in the hour of trial; give them grace to bear faithful witness unto Thee; and endue them with burning zeal and love, that they may turn many to righteousness, and finally obtain a crown of glory; through Jesus Christ, our Lord. *Amen.*

102—*For Missionaries*

O LORD JESUS CHRIST, Who, ascending to Thy throne of glory, didst commission Thy disciples to carry the message of Thy love to every people: As Thou

hast promised to be with Thine own unto the end, vouchsafe
Thy strengthening Presence to all those who have gone
forth and are going forth in Thy Name to strange lands and
peoples; enable them by Thy Spirit to preach, teach, and
live Thee in all Thy love and tenderness, granting them in
the ingathering of souls that inspiration of joy that shall
make them strong to persevere, and to carry their cross in
carrying Thine; Who livest and reignest with the Father, in
the unity of the Holy Ghost, One God, world without end.
Amen.

103—*For Medical Missionaries*

O JESUS, our Master, Who didst show the love of God
by healing all manner of sickness and disease, grant
this same love to all the physicians and nurses who are
serving Thee in missionary hospitals and dispensaries, and
to those who are still preparing for this service. Give them
Thy good gifts of wisdom and courage; may they have the
joy of knowing that all the skill and care which they devote
to their work is service truly offered unto Thee. Help them so
to understand and meet the needs of their patients, that their
ministry, by Thy help, may be to the strengthening of their
bodies, the comforting of their spirits, and the healing of
their souls; Who with the Father and the Holy Ghost, livest
and reignest, One God, world without end. *Amen.*

104—*For Medical Missionaries*

O HOLY and Blessed Spirit, Who dost inspire the hearts
of men with good desires: Give, we pray Thee, a lively
sense of the Church's mission of healing to both the bodies
and the souls of men; quicken in us the merciful desire
to alleviate the world's pain and anguish; bless everywhere
the knowledge, skill and faith devoted to this cause; increase the number of those who consecrate their lives to
this service for the sake of Him Who came to heal and to
save, even Jesus Christ, our Lord. *Amen.*

105—*For the Native Church*

O GOD, Who hast spread Thy Church through those whom Thou hast sent into all the world: Be present in Thy grace and power with all those who have come to call Thee Lord, and strengthen the work of Thy growing Church among all peoples far and near, that having called them to the Gospel, they may both live and preach the same, and be one in Christ with all who love and confess His Name; through the Same, Jesus Christ, our Lord. *Amen.*

106—*For the Native Church*

O LORD JESUS CHRIST, great Head of the Church: Keep in Thy mercy Thy growing Church in distant lands; that, having found Thee by Thy Cross and victory, they may be one with all Thy saints in the heritage of the work and maintenance of Thy Kingdom among men; Who livest and reignest with the Father and the Holy Ghost, One God, world without end. *Amen.*

Education

EDUCATION

107—*The Church and Education*

HEAVENLY FATHER, Who art the Source of truth and life and love, we thank Thee for the heritage of learning which has come to us from the past, whereby our knowledge has been increased, our life enriched, and our joy made more abundant. Grant unto us true humility that we may not be disdainful of whatsoever is true in that which is old, nor refuse to receive whatsoever is true in that which is new; but loving Thee with our whole mind, may we rejoice in the accumulation of all true knowledge and use it in the service of our fellowmen, to the glory of Thy Name; through Jesus Christ, our Lord. *Amen.*

108—*For Parish Schools*

O LORD JESUS CHRIST, Who art the eternal Wisdom of the Father: We beseech Thee to assist with Thy heavenly grace the good learning and godly discipline of our children, that in all and above all things they may attain the knowledge of Thee, Whom to know is life eternal; and that, according to the example of Thy holy childhood, as they grow in years they may grow in wisdom, and in favor with God and man; Who livest and reignest with the Father and the Holy Ghost, One God, world without end. *Amen.*

109—*For Parish Schools*

DEAR LORD JESUS, bless, we pray Thee, all who are diligent in Thy worship in Thy house this day. We pray Thee to bless our school. Teach us to understand the blessings and the part we have in Thy Church, and fit us more and more for our daily life, so that we may always be children of Thy Kingdom. *Amen.*

110—*For Parish Schools*

GRANT, O Lord, to all teachers and students, to know that which is worth knowing, to love that which is worth loving, to praise that which pleaseth Thee most, to esteem that which is most precious unto Thee, and to dislike whatsoever is evil in Thine eyes. Grant us with true judgment rightly to distinguish things that differ, and above all to search out and to do what is well-pleasing unto Thee; through Jesus Christ, our Lord. *Amen.*

111—*For Schools of the Church*

ALMIGHTY GOD, Who through Thy Son hast commanded us to teach the nations: We humbly pray Thee to bestow Thy blessing upon the teaching institutions of the Church: its schools, its colleges, its seminaries; and upon all who therein teach and learn; prosper our efforts to guide our youth into the paths of righteousness; raise up consecrated men for Thy holy ministry; and grant us the spirit of true devotion that we may consecrate our gifts to the work of Thy Church, to the glory of Thy holy Name; through Jesus Christ, our Lord. *Amen.*

112—*For Schools of the Land*

ALMIGHTY GOD, of Whose only gift cometh wisdom and understanding: We beseech Thee to behold with Thy gracious favor our universities, colleges, and schools, that knowledge may ever be enlarged and deepened and all good learning flourish and abound. Bless all who teach and all who learn; and grant that both teachers and learners in humility of heart may look ever upward unto Thee, Who art the Fountain of all wisdom; through Jesus Christ, our Lord. *Amen.*

113—*For Schools of the Land*

O GOD, we beseech Thee to bless the schools and universities of the land; root out from them whatever is contrary to true faith and clean morals; grant them the spirit of devotion and humility; make them treasure houses of wholesome learning; awaken them to the consciousness of their responsibility to Thee and to the nation in training our youth to the high ideals of noble, useful living, so that they may be loyal to Thee and faithful citizens of our country; and grant that they may send forth many young men and women to the work of Thy Church at home and abroad, who in unselfish service will ever strive to bring others to Thee; through Jesus Christ, our Lord. *Amen.*

114—*For Schools and Colleges*

O FATHER of lights and Fountain of all knowledge: Bless, we beseech Thee, all teachers and institutions of learning, and grant that through them the light of truth may shine with growing brightness on all men, so that heavenly wisdom and knowledge may be the stability of our times; through Jesus Christ, our Lord. *Amen.*

115—*At the Opening of a Summer School*

O GOD, Who hast sent Thy Son, Jesus Christ, to be the Teacher and Saviour of us all: Bless, we pray Thee, this school, which we begin in Thy Name, this day (*and all that is undertaken therein*); aid those who teach and those who learn; and so renew and increase in us the gifts of Thy Holy Spirit, that we may be built up in our most holy faith, strengthened for every duty, and enabled to render Thee and our fellowmen true and acceptable service; through the Same Jesus Christ, Thy Son, our Lord. *Amen.*

116—*For Theological Seminaries*

O GOD, Who, through Thy Holy Spirit, dost illuminate the minds and sanctify the lives of those whom Thou dost call to the work of pastors and teachers: Look with Thy favor upon all seminaries for the instruction and discipline of those who are to serve in the sacred ministry of Thy Church; bless those who teach and those who learn, that they may apply themselves with such ready obedience to the law of Thy Son, our Saviour, that they may fulfill their ministry with joy; through the Same Jesus Christ, our Lord. *Amen.*

117—*For Pastors to Students*

O LORD JESUS, Teacher and Saviour of men, Who didst say, Seek and ye shall find, knock and it shall be opened unto you: Grant Thine especial blessing to all pastors of students; give them that holiness of life which shall make them an example for others; enable them to enter into the problems of youth with sympathy and understanding, and to lead eager and inquiring minds beyond the things which are seen and temporal to the things which are unseen and eternal; Who livest and reignest with the Father and the Holy Ghost, One God, world without end. *Amen.*

118—*For Pastors to Students*

O GOD of youth, and childhood, and of all men, to remember Whom in the growing years of life is to know the way to eternal joy: Grant that those whom Thou hast sent to minister to the youth in institutions of learning may establish their lives upon the eternal foundations of righteousness, truth, and love, revealed in the holy life and teachings of Thy Son; to the end that they may be kept in communion with Thee in Thy Church; be enabled to live unto Thee in all pleasing, and be prepared for fruitful service to all men in their own day and generation; through the Same, Thy Son, Jesus Christ, our Lord. *Amen.*

119—*For Teachers*

O GOD, Who, through the ministry of Thy chosen ones, hast deigned to reveal unto us the truth of Holy Scripture and hast made us participants in the mysteries of Thy sacraments: Grant to all pastors and teachers, we beseech Thee, that ever coming to Thee, the Fountain of life, and learning of Thee, the eternal Truth, they may reveal to us the way of life and teach us to live in the light of Thy truth; through the Same Jesus Christ, our Lord. *Amen.*

120—*For Teachers*

O LORD JESUS, Who didst take little children in Thy arms and bless them: Grant unto us so to love and tenderly protect the children committed to our care, that by word and example we may bring them to Thee, and teach them to know and love Thee and trust in Thy protection; Who livest and reignest with the Father and the Holy Ghost, One God, world without end. *Amen.*

121—*For Teachers*

O GOD, our Father, Who hast established Thy Kingdom here in earth that men may be drawn to Thee and learn Thy love in Jesus, our Lord; and Who hast committed the teaching of Thy truth and way to Thy Church: We thank Thee for the blessed fellowship of learning hearts which Thou hast established here in this our school and for the holy truth which Thou art teaching us in this Thy house; we thank Thee for those who lead and instruct us in Thy way; and we beseech Thee enrich their lives with the gifts of Thy gracious Spirit so that they may teach us truly and by their faithful example lead us in the way of true living; through Jesus Christ, Thy Son, our Lord. *Amen.*

122—*For Teachers*

O LORD JESUS CHRIST, Who didst come to teach men the heavenly truth that they might brighten life's way with holiness of living: Let Thy truth, Thy way, Thy life be the teaching of our schools; let love for Thee fill the hearts of all who guide and foster our youth; let faith in Thee be their constant, living confession before men, so that our young manhood and womanhood may ever behold in their preceptors Thy blessed example and in their words Thy living teaching, and by Thy grace find in loyal service to Thee the fullness of life; Who with the Father and the Holy Ghost, livest and reignest, One God, world without end. *Amen.*

123—For Teachers

OUR FATHER in Heaven, we thank Thee for the great company of men and women who have dedicated their lives to the children and youth of this generation. We rejoice in their comradeship and thank Thee for their loyalty and devotion. Give them, we pray Thee, Thy blessing. Sanctify them by Thy truth and strengthen them in faith that endures, so that they may guide and inspire others engaged in the work of Christian nurture. Counsel them with Thine eye; shield them from danger; attend them with Thy Presence; and grant them Thy peace. As they share their life with our children, may we co-operate with them in work and intercession, in love and loyalty. Make us with them, we pray Thee, a mighty host of friendship for the furtherance of Thy Kingdom. We ask it in Jesus' Name. *Amen.*

124—For Teachers—For Personal Use

ALMIGHTY GOD, our Heavenly Father, without Whose help labor is useless, without Whose light search is vain: Invigorate my studies, and direct my inquiries, that I may, by due diligence and right discernment, establish myself and others in Thy holy faith. Take not, O Lord, Thy Holy Spirit from me; let not evil thoughts have dominion in my mind. Let me not linger in ignorance, but enlighten and support me, for the sake of Jesus Christ, our Lord. *Amen.*

125—For Teachers in Missionary Schools and Colleges

BLESSED LORD, Who didst condescend to become our Saviour and Teacher: Grant unto all those who labor in mission schools and colleges, aptness to teach and wisdom to win the souls committed to their care. May the seed of Thy Word sown by them in many hearts spring up unto eternal life. May those who are taught seek Thee early and find Thee, their only Saviour and Lord, so that there may be raised up in all lands godly men and women to bear witness unto Thee, Who art God over all, blessed for ever. *Amen.*

126—*For Those Who Teach in Secular Schools*

ALMIGHTY GOD, the Fountain of all wisdom, the Source of all good, Whom to know is everlasting life: We humbly beseech Thee to receive our prayers and supplications for those who teach in the schools of the land: that as they impart to their students such knowledge as will fit them for their stations in life; so by word and example they may also lead them to an appreciation of spiritual things and to the beauty of the life which is lived in Thee; through Jesus Christ, our Lord. *Amen.*

127—*For Students—For Boys and Girls*

O LORD JESUS CHRIST, Who didst yield obedience to Thine elders when Thou wast a boy upon earth: We humbly pray Thee to have mercy upon our boys and girls at school and to prepare them for the work to which Thou wilt call them. Grant that the temptations of youth may not destroy the hopes of their mature life. Make them humble and loving, teachable and diligent. Deliver them from all irreverence, doubt, and hardness of heart; from anger and intemperance; from impurity, whether of mind or body; from dishonesty and falsehood; from sloth; from covetousness and discontent. And so fit them for Thy service and hold them faithful to Thee that they may receive now and in the world to come the blessings of the pure in heart; Who with the Father and the Holy Ghost, livest and reignest, One God, world without end. *Amen.*

128—*For Students*

MOST GRACIOUS GOD, Heavenly Father, Whom to know is life everlasting; remember now, we beseech Thee, those who in the schools of our land seek after wisdom. Save and deliver them from loneliness and despair. Strengthen them in times of weakness. Be Thou the joy of all their pleasures. Grant, at the end of their labors, they may both know and acknowledge Thy Son, Jesus Christ, to

be King of kings and Lord of lords, that going out into
life, their lives may perfectly show forth Thy praise;
through the Same Jesus Christ, Thy Son, our Lord. *Amen.*

129—*For Students*

LORD JESUS CHRIST, our Master Teacher, Who hast
ever led Thy children into truth, grant Thy abiding
Presence unto our sons and daughters in the schools of the
Church; be Thou their Friend and Teacher, their Inspiration and Strength. Give them the habit of Thy humility, the
courage of Thy faith, the comfort of Thy love. Guide and
guard their hearts and minds that they may truly grow in
wisdom and stature and in favor with God and man. Bring
them into a deeper understanding and a richer appreciation
of the faith; so that, loyal to Thy Church, they may love
Thee truly and serve Thee faithfully. For Thy Name's
sake. *Amen.*

130—*For Students*

FATHER in Heaven, Who hast endowed Thy children
with minds and hearts that can respond to the glories
of Thy creation: Grant to the youth of Thy Church, as they
prepare for lives of usefulness, a growing understanding of
their Christian heritage, that learning to know and love
Thee, as Thou hast revealed Thyself in Jesus, our Lord,
their lives may be filled with joy and hope in believing and
serving; through the Same Jesus Christ, our Lord. *Amen.*

PERSONAL PRAYERS FOR THE USE OF STUDENTS

131

O GOD, Who hast given to *me* life with its daily privileges and opportunities: Keep *me* now in the days of
my youth in faithful remembrance of Thee, *my* Creator and
Father. Grant *me* such measure of Thy grace, that *I* may
apply *my* heart to seeking the gifts of Thy eternal wisdom,
so that guided by Thee, *I* may rightly divide truth from
error, the useful from the hurtful. Aid *me* to grow in knowl-

edge and understanding, in strength and every good purpose, so that *I* may live usefully in *my* place as one who know*eth* that life and the privilege of service are from Thee and return to Thee. Hear *me*, *I* pray Thee, in the Name of Thy dear Son, Jesus Christ, my Lord. *Amen.*

132

JESUS, Master, Who only hast the words of eternal life; Who Thyself alone art life's clear, sure way: Number *me* with Thy band of disciples, and there, daily, let *me* go to school with Thee; and that *I* may truly learn, fill *me* with the joy of Thy life; and that *I* may surely know, instruct *me* in the blessed knowledge of Thy truth; so only may *I* be prepared and equipped for life's way and learn to value those things which are high and holy and truly serviceable; to judge fairly and desire sincerely; and by Thy grace determine to possess only such things as are abiding. By Thy example, by the ministration of Thy Spirit, by the inspiration of Thy assured companionship, so hearten *me* to use *my* every gift that *my* life may bring forth the fruitage of true discipleship; for Thy Name's sake. *Amen.*

133

O OUR FATHER, Whose Son, our Lord, grew from childhood to youth to manhood, ever increasing in wisdom and strength and grace and Thy favor: Teach us to number our days and count our every present opportunity, that we may apply our hearts unto wisdom; and as the beginning of this is in Thy fear and the attainment thereof is in Thy favor, grant us such love for Thee that we may devote our minds and gifts to Thy praise in a life of usefulness; through the Same Jesus Christ, Thy Son, our Lord. *Amen.*

134

ALMIGHTY GOD, Who art the Source of all wisdom: Prosper and direct me in my studies, that they may redound to Thy glory and to my eternal good; through Jesus Christ, our Lord. *Amen.*

135—*For Theological Students*

O LORD JESUS CHRIST, bless, we beseech Thee, all those who are preparing for the work of the ministry in Thy holy Church. Remove far from them the spirit of worldliness, and give them grace, that they may continually grow in that holiness of life, which is required of those who bear the vessels of the Lord. Give them that wisdom which cometh from above, and that gentleness which becometh the gospel of peace. Make them diligent in the study of Thy Word, and teach them by Thy Spirit so that they may be enabled to teach others. And so bless them in the years of preparation that they may be thoroughly furnished unto every good work, doing all things unto Thy glory, Who, with the Father and the Holy Ghost, art One God, world without end. *Amen.*

136—*For Those Who Have Gone Forth from Our Schools*

A LMIGHTY GOD, Heavenly Father, Who dost grant gifts to men and grace to use them, bless, we pray Thee, all those who have gone forth from our schools, that they may be accounted worthy stewards of the trust which hath been committed unto them. Keep them in remembrance of the high purposes with which they set forth; let neither failure nor disappointment quench the fire of their zeal or the ardor of their devotion; give unto them true discernment and steadfastness of purpose that, disdaining all that is unworthy and false, they may spend their lives in joyful and unselfish service, glorifying Thee through their love for their fellowmen; through Jesus Christ, our Lord. *Amen.*

137—*For Those Who Have Gone Forth from Our Schools*

D EAR LORD, we thank Thee for our days at school; for all who planned its beginnings and built its halls; for the men who taught and influenced us: We thank Thee for the good foundations there laid to equip us for life's day and service. Keep alive in our hearts the inspiration and joy with which we went forth in days gone by and faced life; and help us to treasure our memories and the blessings of our training, so that we may be worthy to serve in our various walks of life to Thy praise; through Jesus Christ, Thy Son, our Lord. *Amen.*

138—*For Benefactors and the Grace of Giving*

ALMIGHTY GOD, our Father, Who alone art the Author and Giver of all good gifts: Accept, we beseech Thee, our hearty thanks and praise for the labors and blessed memory of the founders of this institution, for its benefactors and for all who, by their gifts, their labors, or their prayers, have befriended it. Raise up, we pray Thee, many sons and daughters in Thy Church to give freely of their substance according to its need for its growth and strengthening; give its teachers wisdom and all needful grace; and be pleased to bless it richly in all things temporal and spiritual as a nursery of faith, knowledge, and zeal for Thy cause among men; through our Lord and Saviour, Jesus Christ. *Amen.*

Home and Friends

HOME AND FRIENDS

139—*The Church and Family Life*

O GOD, Who hast ordained that man should not live alone but in the blessed fellowship of the family life. Grant unto Thy Church that it may continually serve to the strengthening of the family tie through the ministry of the grace of Thy pure love; so that, as they are drawn to Thee, husband and wife, parents and children, may be drawn to one another; through Jesus Christ, our Lord. *Amen.*

140—*For the Family*

O GOD, OUR FATHER, give us homes blessed and hallowed by Thy Presence, that devotion to Thee may unite all who dwell therein, that mutual love may glorify them, that contentment may abide there, that the noble things of life may ever be set before them; so that under Thy protection they may be preserved in the way of life.

Give us godly parents, who by Thy grace may live in faith toward Thee and in love and peace toward all others, inspired by the joy and sacrifice of Thy Fatherhood to nurture their children in Thy faith and fear, and train them to ready service in home and life.

Give us godly children that by Thy grace they may love Thee, and love and honor their parents and reverence their elders, and, inspired by the full obedience of Thy Son and His grace and holiness of life, may they grow from youth to a manhood that will ever enrich the world in which they live and serve; through the Same Thy Son, Jesus Christ, our Lord. *Amen.*

141—*For the Home*

O GOD, Who art our Dwellingplace in all generations: Let Thy blessing rest upon the home, that, illumined by the light of Thy Presence and sanctified by the joy of Thy love, it may be a shelter for the defenseless, a bulwark

for the tempted, a restingplace for the weary, and a fore-
taste of our eternal home in Thee; through Jesus Christ,
our Lord. *Amen.*

142—*For Fathers*

ALMIGHTY FATHER, Who wast well-pleased with Thine
Only-begotten and Well-beloved Son, and Who, in
the home, hast laid upon parents many and important
duties: Mercifully grant to all fathers the wisdom and love
required in their station, and grace to walk faithfully in
Thy sight, that by their good example they may guide
their children in Thy way, and, not provoking them to
wrath, bring them up in the nurture and admonition of
the Lord; through the Same Jesus Christ, our Lord. *Amen.*

143—*For Fathers*

O GOD, the Father Almighty, Creator of heaven and
earth, Who dost preserve the human race through the
family: Give needed grace to all fathers that they may be
faithful to their paternal responsibilities and be useful to
Thee; and, dwelling continually in mutual confidence with
all members of their families, may they worthily receive
the honor of their children; through Jesus Christ, our
Lord. *Amen.*

144—*For Mothers*

O LORD JESUS CHRIST, Who didst love Thy Mother:
Bless, we beseech Thee, and keep in Thine eternal
love all mothers, and especially our own, whom we remember before Thee this day; and grant that we, whom
they have taught Thy way from childhood, may, by our
fruitful lives, ever be a blessing to them; Who with the
Father and the Holy Ghost, livest and reignest, One God,
world without end. *Amen.*

145—*That Marriage May Be Held in Honor by All*

O GOD, Who didst ordain marriage for the good of
mankind, and hast commanded that it be held in
honor by all: Grant that the youth of the land may ever
regard with reverence the sacred ordinance of marriage,

so that with pureness of mind and holiness of life they may approach the time when they shall plight their troth before Thee, and enter upon a life's companionship blessed by Thee; through Jesus Christ, our Lord. *Amen.*

146—*That Marriage May Be Held in Honor by All*

O LORD JESUS CHRIST, Who in the mystery of Thy sacrificial love for the Church didst reveal the mystery of the union of man and woman in marriage: Let Thy blessing rest upon those who are living together in holy wedlock; keep them in remembrance of their solemn vows, so that enabled by Thy love, they may never cease to love and honor each other; and serving Thee with a pure faith, may together become heirs of the grace of life; Who with the Father and the Holy Ghost, livest and reignest, One God, world without end. *Amen.*

147—*Neighbors*

O UR HEAVENLY FATHER, Who dost surround our daily life with familiar things and well-known faces, and dost teach us to love our neighbor as ourself: We pray for all those among whom we live, our neighbors and acquaintances; for those with whom we work; for those whose lives ours will touch as we pass through the day's tasks and privileges; as well as for our dearest friends and near relations, humbly committing them all to Thy favor and care, beseeching Thee to guard and preserve them and us from all dangers of body and soul, that, by Thy grace and ever present help, we may so live now that we may dwell with Thee in the life that knows no ending; through Jesus Christ, our Lord. *Amen.*

148—*For Children*

O BLESSED and Loving Saviour Jesus Christ, Who at Nazareth didst reveal the beauty of perfect childhood, and in the days of Thy ministry didst call the little ones unto Thee and bless them: Look upon the children of the

Church and nation, and grant that in homes and schools, sanctified by Thy Presence and devoted to Thy glory, they may grow up in the love and in the fear of Thee, and in the knowledge of the true faith, through the grace of the indwelling Spirit, Who, with Thee and the Almighty Father, liveth and reigneth, One God, for ever and ever. *Amen.*

149—*For Children*

O LORD JESUS CHRIST, Who art the eternal Wisdom of the Father: We beseech Thee to assist with Thy heavenly grace the good learning and godly discipline of our children, that in all and above all things they may attain the knowledge of Thee, Whom to know is life eternal; and that, according to the example of Thy childhood, as they grow in years they may grow in wisdom and in favor with God and man; hear us, we pray, for Thy Name's sake. *Amen.*

150—*For Children*

OUR FATHER, we thank Thee that Thou hast blessed us and brightened our home with children; and we humbly pray that they with us may always be numbered in Thy Family. Teach them and guide them day by day that they may learn and walk in the way of righteousness; protect and foster them that they may be guarded from all evil and strengthened to overcome every temptation; fill their minds with high ideals, their hearts with purity, love and holy purpose, that they may consecrate themselves to Thy service and ever remain true in their allegiance; let them learn the responsibility of Thy trust and of daily duty; and fit them for a life of usefulness, so that they may render to Thee a good accounting of the life Thou hast entrusted to their stewardship. This we humbly ask for them in the Name of Thy dear Son. *Amen.*

151—*For Friends*

O GOD, Who, through the grace of the Holy Spirit, dost pour the gifts of love into the hearts of the faithful: Grant unto all our friends, Thy servants, for whom we entreat Thy clemency, health of mind and body; so that they may love Thee with all their strength, and in gladness accomplish all things pleasing unto Thee; through Jesus Christ, our Lord. *Amen.*

152—*For Friends and Near Ones*

WE give thanks unto Thee, Heavenly Father, that Thou hast kept us this day in Thy care; remember those who have borne with us the burden and heat of the day, and enrich their lives with the things which perish not; guard the workers of the night, keeping far from them the powers of darkness. Bless our friends, and neighbors, and especially those most dear to us. Bless, O Lord, we earnestly pray Thee, . . .;* all those who are in any wise committed to our care; grant them health of soul and body; preserve them from sin and error; make them Thy faithful servants; and defend them evermore with Thy heavenly grace; through Jesus Christ, our Lord. *Amen.*

153—*For Friends in Need*

O ALMIGHTY SPIRIT, Comforter, most perfect Consoler of them that mourn: Enter, we beseech Thee, by Thy mighty power into the innermost sanctuary of the hearts of those who sorely need Thee, and of Thy goodness dwell therein, making them glad with the brightness of Thy glorious light, that they may be strengthened to persevere in the service of Jesus Christ, our Lord. *Amen.*

154—*For Absent Brethren and Friends*

ALMIGHTY FATHER, Who art present in Thy power in every place: Give ear in Thy loving-kindness to the supplications which we offer unto Thee on behalf of our brethren and friends now absent from us; may Thy mighty

---

*NOTE: *Here may be mentioned by name any for whom it is desired to pray, such as, children, family, absent ones, etc.*

hand shield and protect them from all evil; may Thy Holy Spirit guide them in the right way and bless their going out and their coming in; (*bring them back to us in safety*), and grant that, being united by our fellowship with Thee, we may all at the last be gathered in the home which is above; through Jesus Christ, our Lord. *Amen.*

155—*For Absent Brethren and Friends*

O GOD, before Whose altar there is neither far nor near but one eternal Presence: We commend to Thy gracious keeping all everywhere whom Thou hast united with ourselves in bonds of love and friendship, beseeching Thee, that as we pray for them they also may pray for us, and that Thou mayest maintain them and us in holy and blessed fellowship; through Jesus Christ, our Lord. *Amen.*

156—*For Absent Brethren and Friends*

O LORD GOD ALMIGHTY, Who dwellest in love and abidest in peace; of Whose gift it cometh that the bond of affection is not severed by separation, but rather increased by the longing of remembrance: We pray and beseech Thee, that in us may remain true and pure that unwearied love which always cherishes the absent ones and does not exclude from the heart those who are far away; through Thy mercy, O our God, Who art blessed for evermore. *Amen.*

157—*For the Absent*

O GOD, our Heavenly Father, Who art everywhere present alike with them that are afar off and them that are nigh: We commend to Thy gracious keeping our friends, now absent from us; beseeching Thee to preserve them from danger, to uphold them in hours of sadness, and ever to direct their way in the paths of righteousness; that, having Thee for their Protector and Guide, they may pass through this present life in safety and in peace; through Him, Who is the way, the truth, and the life, Jesus Christ, our Lord. *Amen.*

Gifts and Graces

GIFTS AND GRACES

158—*Communion with God*

O GOD of Peace, Who hast taught us that in returning
and rest we shall be saved, that in quietness and confidence shall be our strength: By the might of Thy Spirit
lift us, we pray Thee, to Thy Presence, where we may be
still and know that Thou art God; through Jesus Christ,
Thy Son, our Lord. *Amen.*

159—*Communion with God*

B LESSED FATHER, in the Name and Spirit of Him
Who is Thy love and our way to Thee, we lift up our
hearts to praise and adore Thee, and in holy stillness to
wait on Thee: And as only the pure in heart may see Thee,
cleanse our hearts that they may be fit to worship and
receive Thee; attune our souls to Thy holy grace that as
Thou speakest to us, we may gladly hear: that as we speak
to Thee, we may rejoice to know Thou art glad to hear and
receive our prayer; so may we find in sacred communion
with Thee strength for our day and way, and grace to walk
before Thee in holiness and peace; through the Same Jesus
Christ, our Lord. *Amen.*

160—*Communion with God*

O HEAVENLY FATHER, Who through Thy Son, Jesus
Christ, hast brought us to sonship with Thyself: Send,
we beseech Thee, the Spirit of Thy Son continually into our
hearts, that amid all our striving to know and do Thy will,
we may not lose the consciousness that Thou art ever near
us to support our weakness, to increase our strength, and
to satisfy our need; and grant that by Thy Spirit we may
have grace ever to call Thee by Thy Name, crying, Abba,
Father; through the Same Jesus Christ, our Lord. *Amen.*

161—*To Feel the Nearness of God*

HELP US, O God, to feel Thy nearness to the world and to ourselves; help us to remember that Thou art never far away, but always with us, in joy and sorrow, in happiness and pain, and that even when we sin, Thou still art close to us; and grant that thus knowing Thee to be with us, we may be strengthened to do Thy will; through Jesus Christ, our Lord. *Amen.*

162—*For a Right Knowledge of God*

O GOD, Who dost put into the hearts of men longings that they can neither understand nor satisfy without Thine aid: Make us to have a strong desire to know Thee as Thou art, in all Thy goodness, purity, and truth; and grant, we beseech Thee, that we may find that desire fulfilled in Thy Son, Jesus Christ, our Lord. *Amen.*

163—*For a Right Knowledge of God*

O GOD, Who in the days of old didst make Thyself known to prophets and poets, and in the fullness of time didst reveal Thyself in Thy Son, Jesus Christ: Help us so to meditate upon the revelation of Thyself which Thou hast given, that Thy constant love may become known to us, and we may feel Thy Presence always with us; through the Same Jesus Christ, our Lord. *Amen.*

164—*For Grace to Live Aright*

ALMIGHTY GOD, Who alone gavest us the breath of life, and Who by Thy Spirit dost keep alive in us all holy desires: We beseech Thee, for Thy compassion's sake, to sanctify all our thoughts and endeavors, so that we may neither begin an action without a pure intention nor continue it without Thy blessing, but walking with Thee this day we may both purpose and accomplish that which is wholly pleasing to Thee; through Jesus Christ, Thy Son, our Lord. *Amen.*

165—*For Grace to Live Aright*

O GOD, Who, by the example of Thy dear Son hast warned us that we should work Thy works while it is day, before the night cometh, when no man can work; keep us from sloth and idleness, and from the misuse of those talents which Thou hast committed to our trust. Enable us to perform the several duties of our estate and calling with such care and diligence that our work may never be reproved in Thy sight. And forasmuch as the needful business of this life is apt to steal away our hearts from Thee, give us grace to remember that we have a Master in heaven, and to do everything in singleness of heart, as unto Thee and not unto men, that of Thee we may receive the reward of the inheritance which Thou hast promised in Thy Son, our Saviour, Jesus Christ. *Amen.*

166—*For Grace to Live Aright*

O LORD GOD, lead us away from the way of iniquity, and teach us to love Thy law, that removing from us the habit of sinning Thou mayest inspire us to persevere in right living; through Thy mercy, O our God, Who art blessed for evermore. *Amen.*

167—*For Grace to Live Aright*

MOST MERCIFUL FATHER, open our hearts, we beseech Thee, and grant us to desire with ardent mind those things which please Thee, to search for them wisely, to know them truly, and to fulfill them perfectly, to the honor and glory of Thy holy Name; through Jesus Christ, our Lord. *Amen.*

168—*For Spiritual Refreshment*

O LORD JESUS CHRIST, with Whom is the fountain of life, give us all, we entreat Thee, grace and good will to follow the leadings of Thy most Holy Spirit. Let the dew of Thy grace descend and abide upon us, refreshing that which droops, reviving that which is ready to perish; until the day when all Thy faithful people shall be satisfied with the fatness of Thy house, and drink of the river of Thy pleasures. *Amen.*

169—*For Consecration*

O LORD JESUS CHRIST, Who didst send forth Thy disciples to preach glad tidings of the Gospel, and didst command that it be taught to all men, we thank Thee for the unbroken line of faithful witnesses through whom it has come to us, and that we, though the least of Thy saints, may serve Thee in the same holy calling. Grant we implore Thee, to us and to all Thy people, Thy promised grace, that, intent upon fulfilling Thy commission, we may shrink from no labor, withhold no service, and be turned aside by no doubts and discouragements, until Thou dost call us to rejoice in the fruit of our toil in Thy heavenly Kingdom; Who livest and reignest with the Father and the Holy Spirit, One God, world without end. *Amen.*

170—*For Consecration*

O GOD, our God and the God of our fathers, we consecrate to Thee all that we are and all that we have, the powers of our mind, the members of our body, our wealth, and our time: Grant us grace, O Father of mercies, to employ all to Thy glory, and to live in obedience to Thy commands, with an ardent and humble desire to continue Thine throughout the endless ages of eternity; through Jesus Christ, our Lord. *Amen.*

171—*For True Discipleship*

O LORD JESUS CHRIST, Who hast drawn us to Thee and called us into Thy discipleship: Help us to have Thee always before us, in all that we do or think or say; and in every time of testing keep us faithful, knowing that Thou alone hast the words of eternal life; Who livest and reignest with the Father and the Holy Ghost, One God, world without end. *Amen.*

172—*For True Discipleship*

OUR HEAVENLY FATHER, we humbly confess our sins in that we have left undone the things which we should have done, and have done the things we should not have done. Forgive us our sad betrayals, our broken loyalties, our faint attachments to Thy cause. Make us Thy true disciples, enabling us to keep the faith, not to falter nor run away. And bring us all at last to the reward in heaven of those who finish bravely their high calling in Him Who loved us and gave Himself for us, even Jesus Christ, Thy Son, our Lord. *Amen.*

173—*Personal Witnessing*

O JESUS CHRIST, Who art greater than the greatest of the sons of men, before Whom we bow in reverence and adoration; Whom we call Lord and Saviour and Master and Redeemer: Make us Thy faithful witnesses, to carry Thy Gospel to those who know Thee not, to speak Thy truth to those who have not heard it or who have forgotten it, to testify by word and act that Thou art indeed the Son of the living God; Who livest and reignest with the Father and the Holy Ghost, One God, world without end. *Amen.*

174—*Temperate Living*

ALMIGHTY GOD, Lord of angels, Father of men, Who openest Thine hand and fillest all things with plenty: Teach us to use the gifts of Thy providence soberly and temperately, that our temptations may not be too strong for us, nor our affections sensual and unholy. Grant, O Lord, that the blessings which Thou givest us may neither minister to sin nor to sickness, but to health and holiness and thanksgiving; so that in the strength of Thy provision we may faithfully and diligently serve Thee; through Jesus Christ, our Lord. *Amen.*

175—*To Live the Risen Life*

O LORD, Who hast promised a blessing to all who seek first Thy Kingdom and its righteousness: Enlighten our hearts with Thy Holy Spirit, so that He may show us the path of life and the fullness of joy in Thy Presence; and through Him teach us, as those who have risen with Thee, so to set our affections on the eternal pleasures that are above, that our life, even now, may be truly hid with Thee, O Christ, in God our Father, with Whom Thou livest and reignest in the unity of the Holy Spirit, now and evermore. *Amen.*

176—*For Heavenly Mindedness*

O LORD, Whose favor is life, and in Whose Presence there is fullness of peace and joy: Vouchsafe unto us, we beseech Thee, such an abiding sense of the reality and glory of those things which Thou hast prepared for them that love Thee, as may serve to raise us above the vanity of this present world, both in its pleasures and in its necessary trials and pains; so that under Thy guidance and help all things here shall work together for our everlasting salvation; through Jesus Christ, our Lord. *Amen.*

177—*Repentance*

O LORD GOD, Heavenly Father, we pray Thee, lead and direct us by Thy Holy Spirit, so that we may not regard our sins lightly or lose ourselves in over-confidence, but by His grace continually bring forth the fruits of repentance, and endeavor to amend our lives from day to day, always finding sure comfort in that Thou art ever gracious to us, and dost forgive our sins and save us eternally; through Jesus Christ, our Lord. *Amen.*

178—*Forgiveness*

O GOD, Whose goodness is great, and the multitude of Thy mercies innumerable; we have sinned against Thee, and done evil in Thy sight, yet because Thou art the God of mercy and the Fountain of eternal purity we present unto Thee the sacrifice of a troubled spirit, beseeching Thee to let the fire of Thy love cleanse our sins and purify our souls. Make clean our hearts, O God; though our sins be as scarlet, yet make them like wool; though they be as purple, yet make them white as snow. Restore the voice of joy and gladness to us; give us the comforts of Thy help again, and let Thy free Spirit establish us in the liberty of the sons of God: so shall we sing of Thy righteousness, and our lips shall give Thee praise in the congregation of Thy redeemed, now, henceforth, and for ever; through Jesus Christ, our Lord. *Amen.*

179—*Purity (Sanctification)*

O GOD, the Father of our Lord Jesus Christ, Whose Name is great, Whose goodness is inexhaustible, Who art worshiped by the cherubim and adored by the seraphim, before Whom stand ten thousand times ten thousand, the hosts of holy angels and archangels: Sanctify, O Lord, our souls and bodies and spirits, touch our minds and search our consciences and cast out from us every evil thought and impure imagination, all envy and pride, all worldly anxiety and covetousness, all anger and remembrance of injuries, and every motion of body and soul that is contrary to Thy holy will. And grant us, O Lover of men, with freedom and a pure heart, without confusion of face and with hallowed lips, boldly to call upon Thee, our holy God and Father in heaven; through Jesus Christ, our Lord. *Amen.*

180—*Joy in God's Creation*

O HEAVENLY FATHER, Who hast filled the world with beauty: Open, we beseech Thee, our eyes to behold Thy gracious hand in all Thy works; that rejoicing in Thy whole creation we may learn to serve Thee with gladness; for the sake of Him by Whom all things were made, Thy Son, Jesus Christ, our Lord. *Amen.*

181—*For the Ministry of Things Beautiful*

O GOD, Who in Thy holy Word hast commanded us to worship Thee in the beauty of holiness, and Whose glory is great in all the churches: We praise Thy holy Name for the great beauty with which Thou hast clothed Thy creation, for the beauty of the forest and the field, of the sky and the sea, of man and every living thing. We pray Thee to impress upon us the truth of the Gospel through the forms and figures wrought by human hands for the service of Thy house. Grant that they may have a ministry of holiness and loveliness in our lives. Bestow upon us Thy heavenly grace, that we may in all things grow up to the life that is in Christ, Who is fairer than the sons of men, and that our thoughts, words, and works may show forth Thy praise; through the Same Jesus Christ, our Lord. *Amen.*

182—*Love to Our Brethren*

O GOD of Love, Who hast given a new commandment through Thine Only-begotten Son, that we should love one another, even as Thou didst love us, the unworthy and the wandering, and gavest Thy beloved Son for our life and salvation: We pray Thee, Lord, give to us Thy servants, in all time of our life on the earth, a mind forgetful of past ill-will, a pure conscience and sincere thoughts, and a heart to love our brethren; through the Same Jesus Christ, our Lord. *Amen.*

183—*Christian Service*

O LORD, our Heavenly Father, Whose blessed Son came not to be ministered unto, but to minister: We beseech Thee to bless all who, following in His steps, give themselves to the service of their fellowmen. Endue them with wisdom, patience, and courage to strengthen the weak and raise up those who fall; that, being inspired by Thy love, they may worthily minister in Thy Name to the suffering, the friendless, and the needy; for the sake of Him, Who laid down His life for us, Thy Son, our Saviour, Jesus Christ. *Amen.*

184—*Christian Service*

O LORD JESUS CHRIST, Who didst consecrate Thyself wholly to the doing of Thy Father's will: Conform our wills unto Thine; take our hearts and fill them with Thy love; take our lips and speak through them to Thy Kingdom's spread; take our lives and use them to Thy blessed purpose; make us, Lord, vessels of Thy grace, examples of Thy teaching, witnesses of Thy truth and glory; Who livest and reignest with the Father and the Holy Ghost, One God, world without end. *Amen.*

185—*Christian Service*

LORD GOD the Holy Ghost, Comforter and Sanctifier: Take of the things of Christ and show them unto us, that having found all in Him, being built up in faith and filled with His love, we may be enabled to give our whole selves to unselfish service, and find in every task or burden the gladsome blessing of consecration to Father, Son, and Thee; and in every victory over temptation, wrong and sin, the peace of God which passeth understanding; Who livest and reignest with the Father and the Son, One God, world without end. *Amen.*

186—*Fullness of Joy in God's Service*

O OUR FATHER, Whose dear Son, for the joy set before Him, endured the Cross: Do Thou make of our life, as Thou didst make of our Saviour's life, an inspired and controlled and directed obedience, days linked to days, tasks to further tasks, all tending to the fulfillment in us of Thy holy will, so that finding the fullness of joy in Thy service, we may now and evermore rejoice in the hope of the glory of God; through the Same, Jesus Christ, our Lord. *Amen.*

187—*Truth and Honor*

ALMIGHTY GOD, Who hast sent the Spirit of truth unto us to guide us into all truth, so rule our lives by Thy power, that we may be truthful in thought, and word, and deed. O keep us, most merciful Saviour, with Thy gracious protection, that no fear or hope may ever make us false in act or speech. Cast out from us whatsoever loveth or maketh a lie, and bring us all into the perfect freedom of Thy truth; through Jesus Christ, Thy Son, our Lord. *Amen.*

188—*Courage*

O GOD, Who rulest the worlds from end to end and from everlasting to everlasting: Speak to our hearts when courage fails, and men faint for fear, and the love of many grows cold, and there is distress of the nations upon earth. Keep us resolute and steadfast in the things that cannot be shaken, abounding in hope and knowing that our labor is not in vain in Thee. Restore our faith in the omnipotence of good; renew in us the love which never faileth; and make us to lift up our eyes and behold, beyond the things which are seen and temporal, the things which are unseen and eternal; through Jesus Christ, our Lord. *Amen.*

189—*Courage*

TEACH US, good Lord, to serve Thee as Thou deservest, to give and not count the cost: to fight and not heed the wounds: to toil and not seek for rest: to labor and not ask for reward, save that of knowing that we do Thy will; Who with the Father and the Holy Ghost, livest and reignest, One God, world without end. *Amen.*

190—*In Time of Doubt*

O GOD, by Whom the meek are guided in judgment, and light riseth up in darkness for the godly: Grant us, in all our doubts and uncertainties, the grace to ask what Thou wouldest have us to do; that the Spirit of wisdom may save us from all false choice, and that in Thy light we may see light, and in Thy strait path may not stumble; through Jesus Christ, our Lord. *Amen.*

191—*For Trust amid the Perplexities of Life*

O MOST LOVING FATHER, Who willest us to give thanks for all things, to dread nothing but the loss of Thee, and to cast all our care on Thee, Who carest for us: Preserve us from faithless fears and worldly anxieties, and grant that no clouds of this mortal life may hide from us the light of that love which is immortal, and which Thou hast manifested unto us in Thy Son, Jesus Christ, our Lord. *Amen.*

192—*For Constancy in Time of Trial*

O LORD, Who didst pray amidst the shadows of the olive trees, teach us to pray, lest we enter into temptation. Teach us the patience of unanswered prayer, and such an abiding trust in Thy good will that no impatience, no foolish fear, no suffering of the mind or body shall break our faith in Thee. Teach us to say: Thy will be done; to accept Thy will in all things; and to do it as we know it; and out of our shadows, bring us into the light of Thy great love for us and for all mankind, Who with the Father and the Holy Ghost art God, blessed now and evermore. *Amen.*

193—*In Time of Need*

O LORD, our God, we thank Thee for all Thy mercies, but especially for Thy mercy in Christ, our Saviour, Who, because of our sins, felt Himself to be forsaken in the darkness of the Cross, yet at the last committed His Spirit unto Thee. Help us likewise by His great example, in every time of need to commend ourselves to Thy keeping, so that having suffered bravely with Him, our Lord, we may finally rejoice with Him in everlasting life; through the Same, Jesus Christ, our Saviour. *Amen.*

194—*Thankfulness for the Blessings of this Age*

O GOD, of Whom, and through Whom, and to Whom are all things; Whose is the kingdom, and the power, and the glory; Who art Lord of all: yet art Thou our loving Father: Keep us, Thy children, whom Thou hast endowed with wondrous gifts and abilities, ever humble and single in our devotion to Thee, that as we employ the marvelous inventions which men have been permitted to create, whereby in daily life we use the forces and provisions of nature, we may not presume to vaunt our wisdom nor trust in our strength, but bowing before Thee, Who holdest all things in the hollow of Thy hand, give Thee thanks and praise; through Jesus Christ, our Lord. *Amen.*

195—*For Protection*

O GOD, our Heavenly Father, our Refuge and Strength, Who givest Thine angels charge over us to keep us in all our ways: Grant us Thy almighty protection, we beseech Thee, in every danger that threatens the health and peace of our bodies; but especially, we pray Thee, do Thou protect our souls in all spiritual danger; deliver us from the power of our sins; in every temptation grant us Thine aid; make us strong to resist the evil and to choose the good, and save us by Thy grace; through Jesus Christ, Thy Son, our Lord. *Amen.*

196—*For Angelic Guard*

ALMIGHTY, Everlasting God, Who hast created us, who are so unworthy, after Thine own image, and hast appointed Thy holy angels as our guard: Grant us, Thy servants, that guarded by them, we may safely pass through the perils of all evils whether to soul or body, and after this life has run its course, cause us to enter into eternal joy; through Jesus Christ, our Lord. *Amen.*

197—*For Guidance*

JESUS, Master, do Thou meet us while we walk in the way, and long to reach the heavenly country; so that following Thy light, we may keep the way of righteousness, and never wander away into the darkness of this world's night, while Thou, Who art the way, the truth, and the life, art shining within us; through Thy mercy, O our God, Who art blessed for evermore. *Amen.*

Our Daily Life

OUR DAILY LIFE

198—*Before Reading Holy Scripture*

O EVERLASTING GOD and Father of our Lord Jesus
Christ, grant us Thy grace that we may study the
Holy Scriptures diligently, and, with our whole heart, seek
and find Christ therein and through Him obtain everlasting
life; through the Same Jesus Christ, our Lord. *Amen.*

199—*The Study of God's Word*

A LMIGHTY and Most Merciful God, Who hast given Thy
Word to be the revelation of Thy great love to man,
and of Thy power and will to save him: Grant that our
study of it may not be made in vain by the hardness or
carelessness of our hearts, but that by it we may be con-
firmed in penitence, lifted to hope, made strong for service, and above all filled with the true knowledge of Thee
and of Thy Son, Jesus Christ. *Amen.*

200—*For the Right Use of the Scriptures*

O GOD, Who hast made Thyself known to men through
law-givers and prophets and, at last, through Thy
Son, Jesus Christ; and Who hast caused this revelation of
Thyself to be written for our learning: Grant that in these
Holy Scriptures we may find Thee in all Thy glory, Thy
goodness, and Thy love; and help us at all times, and
especially in all times of temptation, to draw from them
comfort and strength and the power of Thy Holy Spirit
for the resistance of evil and the doing of Thy will; through
the Same Jesus Christ, our Lord. *Amen.*

201—*For the Right Use of the Scriptures*

A LMIGHTY GOD, Who hast granted us Thy holy Word
and revealed Thyself to us therein, and through it
dost teach us the way of righteous living: Grant us ever to
reverence, love, and treasure the Holy Scriptures; implant

within us the desire and purpose constantly to read and study them; and as Thou hast promised wisdom to all who seek it, teach us by Thy Holy Spirit wisdom for this earthly life, so that we may grow in grace and in the knowledge of Jesus, our Lord, and be made wise unto salvation; through the Same Jesus Christ, our Lord. *Amen.*

202—*Daily Work*

ALMIGHTY GOD, Who, when Thou didst send forth man from Eden, didst command him to labor in the sweat of his brow: We acknowledge that all our toil and work are in vain without Thy blessing and aid; and we humbly beseech Thee to assist us patiently to fulfill our calling, and faithfully to accomplish our work, graciously enriching it with Thy blessing, in order that the labor of our hands may prosper and in thankfulness we may consecrate the fruits thereof to the spread of Thy Kingdom and the help of the needy; through Jesus Christ, our Lord. *Amen.*

203—*Daily Work*

ALMIGHTY GOD, our Heavenly Father, Who declarest Thy glory and showest forth Thy handiwork in the heavens and in the earth: Deliver us, we beseech Thee, in our several callings, from the service of mammon, that we may do the work which Thou givest us to do in truth, in beauty, and in righteousness, with singleness of heart as Thy servants, and to the benefit of our fellowmen; for the sake of Him Who came among us as one that serveth, Thy Son, Jesus Christ, our Lord. *Amen.*

204—*For Any Undertaking*

ALMIGHTY GOD, the Giver of all good things, without Whose help all labor is insufficient, and without Whose grace all wisdom is folly: Grant, we beseech Thee, that in this our undertaking, Thy Holy Spirit may not be withheld from us, but that we may promote Thy glory, and the coming of Thy Kingdom. Grant this, O Lord, for the sake of Jesus Christ. *Amen.*

205—*For Any Undertaking*

O GOD, from Whom every good thing taketh its beginning and through Whom it gathereth rich growth, always advancing to better things: Grant to us suppliants, we beseech Thee, that this which we undertake to the praise of Thy Name, we may, by the help of Thy Fatherly wisdom, carry through to completion; through Jesus Christ, our Lord. *Amen.*

206—*For Those Who Toil*

O GOD, the Fountain of equity, give to all masters and leaders of industry, faithfulness and truth; to the laboring husbandman, health and fair seasons of the year; to all workers, diligence in their callings and a blessing on their labors; to the prosperous, a liberal heart and an open hand; to all, pardon and holiness and life eternal; through Jesus Christ, our Lord. *Amen.*

207—*For Those Who Toil*

ALMIGHTY and Eternal God, we beseech Thee to bless all the workers of this land. Fulfil all their right desires. Make them faithful in work, loyal in word, and eager for service. Grant that none of them may neglect the call of our Saviour, Jesus Christ, to love Thee in purity, to serve Thee in faithfulness, and to worship Thee in holiness. Keep all evil from their hearts and all mischief from their homes, and draw them nearer to Thee and to one another in the ways of brotherhood and peace; through Jesus Christ, our Lord. *Amen.*

208—*For Those Who Toil*

O GOD, our Heavenly Father, we beseech Thee to hear us on behalf of all who live by the labor of their hands; that they may realize the dignity of toil, with good will doing service as to the Lord and not to men. We pray especially for those who work in dangerous places, or under hard conditions; for those who are oppressed and broken in spirit; for those who are discouraged or who labor without joy or hope. We pray for the unemployed; for those who seek work and find it not; for those who are sick and destitute and suffering, and for those who are without home or friends. Do Thou bless, sustain, protect, and comfort all such, and be to them and to all men a very present Help in time of need; through Jesus Christ, our Lord. *Amen.*

209—*For Those Who Toil*

BLESSED LORD, Who by the example of Thy work at Nazareth hast sanctified our daily toil, and by Thy teaching hast revealed the sympathy of God in our common tasks: Grant that in the midst of our work we may find rest and peace in Thy Presence, and may take joy in all that ministers to Thy service, Who art ever our Refuge, our Strength, and our exceeding great Reward. *Amen.*

210—*For Employers of Labor*

O THOU Who art the Creator of all men and Who wilt judge us all in righteousness: Pour out Thy Spirit, we pray Thee, upon those who have prospered in business, who have great industries under their care, and who employ others to labor under their direction. May they not become vain because of their success, or be exalted above measure because of their prosperity. May they not forget Thee Who givest the power to gain wealth, and Who requirest much of those to whom much is given. May they do justly, love mercy, and walk humbly before Thee, remembering that One is their Master, even Jesus Christ, and that all men are brethren. Teach them so to use their wealth and so to administer their affairs, that they may be a blessing to society and may be able to render unto Thee a good account of their stewardship; through the Same Jesus Christ, our Lord. *Amen.*

211—*For Employers*

O GOD, Merciful and Just: We humbly beseech Thee to sanctify the hearts of those who are in positions of authority and influence, that they may act justly toward all who are in their employ. Keep them from the spirit of oppression and wrong, and from forgetfulness of others. Help them to be tender-hearted to the suffering, liberal to the needy, and in all their dealings considerate and humane. Incline them rightly to use the influence Thou hast given them, that at last they may give an account of their stewardship with joy and thankfulness; through Jesus Christ, our Lord. *Amen.*

212—*For Employers*

O GOD, the Father of all mankind: We beseech Thee for all who employ their fellowmen in all fields of labor; inspire them with such love, truth, and equity, that in all their dealings one with another they may remember that One is their Master, even Thy Son, and may show forth true brotherhood in Thee; through the Same Jesus Christ, our Lord. *Amen.*

213—*For Business and Professional People*

O LORD GOD, Who dost commit unto us the privileges, duties and opportunities of life and dost bid us to occupy till Thou come: Inspire all, who contribute by business or professional activity to our common life, with a high sense of responsibility and with honorable ideals, so that Thy blessing may rest upon their service, and Thou mayest prosper their work and us through them; through Jesus Christ, Thy Son, our Lord. *Amen.*

214—*For Merchants and Tradesmen*

O LORD JESUS CHRIST, Who didst drive the traffickers from the Temple: Bring to failure the efforts of all among us, whether high or low, great or small, who buy and sell dishonestly, who by sharp practices or under the pretext of legal right seek gain at the expense of their fellowmen; and, as Thou didst commend the servants who dealt prudently and honorably, let Thy blessing come upon those who conduct their business honestly and with fair dealing, as those who cherish Thy trust, that they may both prosper and enjoy the honor of a good report; Who livest and reignest with the Father and the Holy Ghost, One God, world without end. *Amen.*

215—*For Husbandmen*

ALMIGHTY GOD, Who hast blessed the earth that it should be fruitful and bring forth abundantly whatsoever is needful for the life of man: Prosper, we beseech Thee, the labors of the husbandman, and grant such seasonable weather that we may gather in the fruits of the earth, and ever rejoice in Thy goodness, to the praise of Thy holy Name; through Jesus Christ, our Lord. *Amen.*

216—*For Seamen*

ALMIGHTY FATHER, with Whom is no distance, and no darkness, and no power too strong for Thy ruling: We beseech Thee to bless on all seas the vessels of our fleet, our sailors and our fishermen, with all that go to and fro and pursue their business in great waters; save them from dangers known or unforseen; deliver them from strong temptation and from easily besetting sin; teach them to mark Thy works and wonders on the deep; fill them with kindness, loyalty and faith, and make every man to do his duty; through Jesus Christ, our Lord. *Amen.*

217—*For Mariners and Fishermen*

O ALMIGHTY GOD, Who madest the sea, and gavest all that moveth therein for the use of man: Bestow Thy blessing, we beseech Thee, on the harvest of the waters that it may be abundant in its season; protect from every peril of the deep all fishermen and mariners, and grant that they may with thankful hearts acknowledge Thee, Who art Lord of the sea and of the dry land; through Jesus Christ, our Lord. *Amen.*

218—*For Miners*

ALMIGHTY GOD, to Whom darkness and light are both alike: Look upon all Thy sons who labor under the earth; keep them mindful of Thy Presence and protect them in their labor; let no evil come near them; save them from all accident and suffering; and grant that they may serve Thee so faithfully in this life, and in the darkness of their labor, that they may at last attain to the brightness of Thy glory; through Him Who gave Himself to labor and suffer for them, Thy Son, Jesus Christ, our Lord. *Amen.*

219—*For Industrial Workers*

ALMIGHTY FATHER, Who by Thy Son hast sanctified labor to the welfare of mankind: Prosper, we pray Thee, the industries of our land and all those who are engaged therein; that, shielded in all of their temptations and dangers, and receiving a due reward of their labors, they may praise Thee by living according to Thy will; through Jesus Christ, our Lord. *Amen.*

220—*For Artisans*

O LORD JESUS CHRIST, Who in Thine own city of Nazareth didst labor with Thy hands, and thus didst hallow all our toil: Look with Thy favor, we pray Thee, upon all craftsmen and workers whose daily occupations supply mankind with things needful for health, comfort and enjoyment. Grant strength to labor and joy in craftsmanship, so that ever striving to prove themselves workmen that need not to be ashamed, and doing all things as unto Thee, all who toil may be conscious of Thy comradeship and have Thy blessing upon all their handiwork; Who livest and reignest with the Father and the Holy Spirit, ever One God, world without end. *Amen.*

221—*For Those Engaged in Scientific Research*

O GOD, the Father Almighty, Maker of heaven and earth and of all things visible and invisible; Whose glory the heavens declare; Whose handiwork the firmament showeth: Grant serious and reverent minds to all who study the marvels of Thy creation and seek to learn the processes of nature for the welfare of mankind; enable them to find in every increase of knowledge new manifestations of Thy divine power, wisdom and love; and as Thou hast created all material things, so do Thou create in us all clean hearts, attune with Thee, to the end that we may be led to know those things which, though not seen, are eternal; through Him Who is truth and life, even Jesus Christ, Thy Son, our Lord. *Amen.*

222—*For Those Whose Toil is Monotonous*

HAVE pity, O Lord God, on all those whose spirit and ambition are blunted by the weariness of monotonous toil; and grant them the cheer of continued faithfulness to duty that arises with the consciousness of all labor well done, be it small or great; hear us and bless them for Thy mercy's sake, O God, through Jesus Christ, our Lord. *Amen.*

223—*For Those Obliged to Work on the Lord's Day*

O LORD, have mercy upon all those who are required to continue in their work upon Thy holy day. Draw their thoughts to Thyself, and make them partakers of the benefits of the prayers and intercessions of Thy holy Church. And grant to their employers grace to consider the needs of those whom Thou hast made in Thine image; that they who toil may not fail at the last to attain that rest which remaineth for the people of God; through Jesus Christ, our Lord. *Amen.*

224—*For Local Industries*

O ALMIGHTY FATHER, Who through Thy Son, Jesus Christ, hast consecrated labor to the blessing of mankind: Prosper, we pray Thee, the industries of this place; defend those who are engaged therein from all perils, and

grant that they may rejoice in the fruits of Thy bounty
and bless Thee for Thy loving-kindness; through the Same
Jesus Christ, our Lord. *Amen.*

225—*For the Unemployed*

O GOD, Who didst send Thy Son, Jesus Christ, to reign
among men: We humbly beseech Thee, establish His
rule in the hearts and lives of men everywhere, so that the
course of this age may be directed according to Thy good
will for all mankind, that every hindrance to the advancement of Thy Kingdom and life in Thee being overthrown,
the whole family of Thy children may be delivered from
heartlessness and greed, from indolence and discontent, and
be enabled to serve Thee and earn their daily bread with
godly joy; through the Same, Thy Son, Jesus Christ, our
Lord. *Amen.*

226—*For the Unemployed*

O OUR FATHER, Whose Son while in the flesh had not
where to lay His head: Look with pity upon all who
seek work and find it not; and of Thy mercy raise up opportunity for their employment, that in peace and thankfulness
they may earn and eat the bread of contentment; for the
sake of Him by Whose poverty we and many are made rich,
even Jesus Christ, our Lord. *Amen.*

227—*For National and Industrial Wellbeing*

O GOD, Who hast cast our lot in a land blessed with
mighty resources, great industries and power: We
praise Thee for Thy goodness toward us, and beseech Thee,
conform to the Spirit of Christ, Thy Son, the wills of all in
whose hand is placed our government, of all who direct the
forces of our business, and of all who administer the
activities of labor; so that our people may live in peace,
perform their daily work in contentment, and eat their bread
with joy and thanksgiving; through the Same Jesus Christ,
our Lord. *Amen.*

228—*For Industrial Peace*

O GOD, Who hast taught us that we are members one of another: Remove, we beseech Thee, from among us all distrust and bitterness in industrial disputes; and grant that, seeking what is just and equal and caring for the needs of others, we may live and work together in unity and love; through Jesus Christ, our Lord. *Amen.*

229—*For Industrial Peace*

O GOD, Who in Thy providence dost appoint to every man His work: We humbly beseech Thee to still all strife and contention amongst those who are engaged in industry (*especially those who are now at variance*); defend them from all greed and covetousness, and grant that they, seeking only that which is just, may live and work together in brotherly union and concord, to their own well-being, and the prosperity of this land; through Jesus Christ, our Lord. *Amen.*

230—*For Social Justice*

ALMIGHTY GOD, Who hast created man in Thine own image: Grant us grace fearlessly to contend against evil, and to make no peace with oppression; and that we may reverently use our freedom, help us to employ it in the maintenance of justice among men and nations, to the glory of Thy holy Name; through Jesus Christ, our Lord. *Amen.*

231—*For the Right Use of Leisure*

O LORD JESUS CHRIST, Who didst call Thy disciples out of their labors to rest awhile, and didst sanctify their rest by Thy Presence: Be present, we pray Thee, with us in our hours of leisure, that guarded against every temptation and preserved from every evil, we may redeem the time by seeking those things which are profitable and enduring. Teach us to see the glory of Thy world, and grant us a spirit to value the noble works of men. Create in our hearts a love of that which is right; give us true discern-

ment, that we may prove all things and hold fast to that
which is good; guard our lips from speaking evil and our
eyes from seeking sin; and so refresh us with Thy Presence
that, renewed in body and mind, we may return to our daily
task contented and at peace; Who livest and reignest with
the Father and the Holy Ghost, One God, world without
end. *Amen.*

232—*Holiday and Travel*

O LORD, be with those who at this season take needful
rest and change from daily toil. Let Thy Presence
brighten their holiday. Preserve them from sin and grant
them renewed strength in body and mind for life's daily
duties; for the sake of Jesus Christ, our Lord. *Amen.*

233—*Holiday and Travel*

A LMIGHTY, Everlasting God, Who didst command the
blessed Apostle Peter to come to Thee walking upon
the sea: Be present with Thy servants voyaging upon the
sea and trusting in Thy mercy; so that by Thy help they
may reach their destination, and, in health and uninjured,
come to a safe haven without hindrance; through Jesus
Christ, our Lord. *Amen.*

234—*Holiday and Travel*

O ALMIGHTY GOD, Whose way is in the sea and whose
paths are in the great waters: Be present, we beseech
Thee, with our brethren in the manifold dangers of the
deep; protect them from all its perils, prosper them in their
course; and bring them, with a grateful sense of Thy
mercies, in safety to the haven where they would be;
through Jesus Christ, our Lord. *Amen.*

235—*For Travelers*

O GOD, Who art everywhere present and Who knowest
our going out and our coming in: We pray for Thy
blessing upon all who travel by land or water or air. Keep
them in safety amid all perils; shield them from tempta-

tion; prosper them in all lawful endeavors; and, by Thy mercy, bring them again in safety to their homes; through Jesus Christ, our Lord. *Amen.*

236—*For Those Who Travel by Air*

ETERNAL GOD, Whose almighty power hath created, and Who ordereth, this world in which we live; Whose all-guarding love surroundeth Thy children in all their goings and comings: Into Thy keeping we commit all those who travel by air and all whose daily tasks bring them into the perils of the places above the earth, that Thou, without Whose knowledge not even a sparrow falleth, mayest preserve them from all harm and accident to body and life; and as they fly through the realms above the earth, uplift their hearts to Thee in trust and praise; through Jesus Christ, Thy Son, our Lord. *Amen.*

237—*For Those Who Travel by Air*

O GOD, Creator and Upholder of all things; Who by Thy wisdom and power hast enabled men by invention and skill to adventure the regions above the earth: We beseech Thee, Who art present everywhere, keep in Thy sustaining care all who travel by air, or whose duty or employment is in this service, that they may enjoy the safety of Thy protection and now and always praise Thee for Thy fatherly love; through Jesus Christ, Thy Son, our Lord. *Amen.*

Special Necessities

SPECIAL NECESSITIES

238—*For the Sick*

ALMIGHTY and Immortal God, Giver of life and health: We beseech Thee to hear our prayers for Thy servant *N.*, for whom we implore Thy mercy, that by Thy blessing upon *him* and upon those who minister to *him* of Thy healing gifts, *he* may be restored to soundness of health, and give thanks to Thee in Thy holy Church; through Jesus Christ, our Lord. *Amen.*

239—*For the Sick*

O FATHER of mercies and God of all comfort, our only Help in time of need: We humbly beseech Thee to behold, visit, and relieve Thy sick *servant* (*N.*) for whom our prayers are desired. Look upon *him* with the eyes of Thy mercy; comfort *him* with a sense of Thy goodness; preserve *him* from the temptations of the enemy; and give *him* patience under *his* affliction. In Thy good time, restore *him* to health, and enable *him* to lead the residue of *his* life in Thy fear and to Thy glory; and grant that finally *he* may dwell with Thee in life everlasting; through Jesus Christ, our Lord. *Amen.*

240—*For the Sick*

O LORD JESUS CHRIST, Who chastenest whom Thou lovest: Grant us grace, we pray Thee, to discern Thy love in whatever suffering Thou sendest us; support us in patient thankfulness under pain, anxiety, or loss; and move us with pity and tenderness for our afflicted neighbors; for Thy mercy's sake. *Amen.*

241—*For One Who is Suffering*

O GRACIOUS FATHER, Whose dear Son bore for us unspeakable agonies, being scourged and crowned with thorns, and nailed to the Cross: Have mercy on Thy servant who is in great suffering, and grant *him* grace to fix *his* eyes upon Thy Son and to conform *himself* to His example, Who for the joy that was set before Him endured the Cross; so that following *his* Master through suffering *he* may attain to His Presence in eternal glory; through the Same Jesus Christ, our Lord. *Amen.*

242—*For One Who is Suffering*

O GOD, Who ever governest Thy creatures with a gracious will: Incline Thy ear to our supplications and look in mercy upon Thy servant who suffereth such great infirmity of body; visit *him* with Thy salvation, and as Thou dost grant *him* health, strengthen *him* with the medicine of heavenly grace; through Jesus Christ, our Lord. *Amen.*

243—*In Time of Great Suffering*

L ORD JESUS CHRIST, our Saviour, Who for man didst bear the Agony and the Cross: Draw Thou near to Thy servant (*servants*) who suffers pain or trouble of mind, so hallowing to *him his* cross that *he* may by Thy grace know that the sufferings of this present time are not worthy to be compared with the glory that shall be revealed; Who with the Father and the Holy Ghost, livest and reignest, One God, world without end. *Amen.*

244—*In Time of Great Suffering*

O GOD, rich in pity as in power, merciful and mighty: Have respect unto Thy whole creation, groaning and travailing in pain until now; and as Thou hast broken the power of evil by the Cross of Christ, and by His endless sacrifice takest away the sin of the world, hasten the time when the last enemy of man shall be trodden under foot, and death shall be no more, neither mourning, nor crying, nor pain, and Thou shalt wipe away all tears from our eyes; through Thy redeeming love in Jesus Christ, our Saviour. *Amen.*

245—*For Those Who Suffer Injury by Accident*

O GOD, our Father, Who through Thy Son didst minister to the sick and broken in body: Mercifully minister to those who, by cause of accident (*this day*), suffer injury of body and anguish of mind; and direct them by Thy Spirit, that as they pray Thee to heal their broken bodies, so they may bring to Thee broken hearts to be made whole by Thy grace in Jesus Christ, our Lord. *Amen.*

246—*In Time of Affliction*

LORD, Thou knowest the deep places through which our lives must go: Help us, when we enter them, to lift our hearts to Thee; help us to be patient when we are afflicted, to be humble when we are in distress; and grant that the hope of Thy mercy may never fail us and the consciousness of Thy loving kindness may never be clouded or hidden from our eyes; through Jesus Christ, our Lord. *Amen.*

247—*Thanksgiving for Recovery from Sickness*

O GOD, in Whose hand are the issues of life and death; Who by the gracious ministry of Thy Son didst heal the sick and raise the dead: We thank Thee that Thou hast restored this our................(*Father,—Mother,—Friend, etc.*) from the gates of death (*or, from grievous sickness*); and we beseech Thee, that *he* may dedicate the life Thou hast preserved to Thy service, and finally be found worthy to enter the happy abode where sickness and death never come; through Jesus Christ, Thy Son, our Lord. *Amen.*

248—*In Time of Distress*

ALMIGHTY GOD, the Refuge of all that are distressed: Grant unto us that, in all trouble of this our mortal life, we may flee to Thee and find comfort in the knowledge of Thy loving-kindness and tender mercy: that sheltered therein, the storms of life may pass over us, and not shake the peace of God that is within us; through Jesus Christ, our Lord. *Amen.*

249—*In Time of Peril*

ANSWER us when we call, O God of righteousness, for from the ends of the earth will we cry unto Thee when our hearts are overwhelmed. Our fathers cried unto Thee and were delivered, they trusted in Thee and were not ashamed. Arise, O God, plead Thine own cause, and give us help, for vain is the help of man. Make bare Thy holy arm in the eyes of all the nations, and let all the ends of the earth see the salvation of our God. *Amen.*

250—*After Some Fatal Calamity*

HAVE mercy, O Lord, upon all those who have suffered in *the* (*our*) recent calamity. Of Thy love supply their outward need, and grant that the present distress may awaken us all to the dangers amidst which we live and the suddenness with which life may end. Of Thy grace fit us to be helpful to our brethren in suffering and distress, and in all our mutual need and at all times to experience the blessed help of Him Who has promised to be with us always, even unto the end. *Amen.*

251—*After Some Fatal Calamity*

O ALMIGHTY GOD, from Whom is derived our life, both in nature and in grace: Remove from us, we beseech Thee, this visitation which Thou hast permitted to come upon us; and grant that we may not forget those lessons which it is intended to teach, but humble ourselves before Thee in lasting penitence for all things that have separated us from Thee and the healthful operation of Thy laws, and serve Thee to the praise of Thy Name; through Jesus Christ, our Lord. *Amen.*

252—*During a Famine*

O GOD, our Heavenly Father, Who by Thy blessed Son hast taught us to ask of Thee our daily bread: Behold, we beseech Thee, the affliction of Thy people, and send us relief in this our necessity; increase the fruits of the earth by Thy heavenly benediction; and grant that we, receiving with thankfulness Thy gracious gifts, may use them to Thy glory, the relief of those who are needy, and our own comfort; through the Same, Thy Son, Jesus Christ, our Lord. *Amen.*

253—*During an Epidemic*

ALMIGHTY GOD and Heavenly Father, Who for our sins art justly displeased, and yet lovest those whom Thou dost chasten; give us grace truly to repent of all our misdeeds and shortcomings. Assuage now, we humbly beseech Thee, the sore sickness which is among us; give ease to those who suffer; comfort all that mourn; give faith to all; and grant Thy people henceforth to serve Thee in righteousness and true holiness; through Jesus Christ, our Lord. *Amen.*

254—*For Those in Sorrow*

O HEAVENLY FATHER, Whose blessed Son, Jesus Christ, did weep at the grave of Lazarus, His friend: Look, we beseech Thee, with compassion upon those who are now in sorrow and affliction: comfort them, O Lord, with Thy gracious consolations; make them to know that all things work together for good to them that love Thee; and grant them evermore sure trust and confidence in Thy fatherly care; through the Same, Jesus Christ, our Lord. *Amen.*

255—*For All Who Are Troubled*

FATHER of mercies, God of all comfort, have pity upon all who are in any trouble. Vouchsafe unto the sick relief from pain and the healing of their diseases. If Thou hast ordained them unto death, minister unto them the grace of Him Who died that we might live with Him for evermore; and grant them, when they go hence, an abundant entrance into His eternal Kingdom. Comfort the mourners. Confirm them in the hope of glory. Show them the things which Thou hast prepared for them that love Thee. Lift their hearts to the Father's house and the rest that remaineth for the people of God. Deal kindly with the aged,

the feeble, and the little children. Be the Friend of the
desolate, the Portion of the poor, the Strength of the weary
and heavy laden. And teach us all to bear one another's
burdens and so fulfill the law of Christ; for His dear sake.
Amen.

256—*For Those in Affliction and Sorrow*

GOD of all comfort, we commend to Thy mercy all those
upon whom any cross or tribulation is laid:—the
nations which are afflicted with famine, pestilence, or war;
those of our brethren who suffer persecution for the sake
of the Gospel; all such as are in danger by sea or land or
in the air, and all persons oppressed with poverty, sickness
or any infirmity of body or sorrow of mind. We pray par-
ticularly for the sick and afflicted members of this church,
and for those who desire to be remembered in our prayers
(*and for any such known to ourselves, whom we name in
our hearts before Thee*). May it please Thee to show them
Thy fatherly kindness, chastening them for their good, that
their hearts may turn unto Thee and receive perfect consolation and deliverance from all their troubles; for Christ's
sake. *Amen.*

257—*For the Fellowship of Christ's Sufferings*

LORD JESUS, we beseech Thee by the loneliness of Thy
suffering on the Cross, be nigh unto all them that are
desolate in pain or sorrow today; and let the grace of Thy
Presence transform their loneliness into comfort, Who art
the sure Refuge of the weary and heavy laden. *Amen.*

258—*For Answered Prayer*

O GOD, Who dost not permit those who hope in Thee
to be afflicted beyond measure but lendest a pitying
ear to their prayers: We give Thee hearty thanks for the
answer vouchsafed to our petitions, humbly beseeching
Thee, that by Thy grace we may ever praise Thee with
thankful lives, and with trusting hearts gladly present our
daily needs before Thee; through Jesus Christ, our Lord.
Amen.

All Sorts and Conditions of Men

ALL SORTS AND CONDITIONS OF MEN

259—*For One Brotherhood in Christ*

O GOD, Who by Thy Son, Jesus Christ, hast broken down the walls of partition between Jew and Gentile, slave and free, Greek and Barbarian: Break down, we beseech Thee, all that divides us one from another; shame our jealousies, and lay low our pride; do away with all race-prejudice, that the bonds of fellowship and mutual service may unite the east and the west, the north and the south, that we may live in peace together, in honor preferring one another; to the glory of Thy great Name; through Jesus Christ, the Saviour of all men. *Amen.*

260—*For One Brotherhood in Christ*

E TERNAL SPIRIT, through Whom in every nation he that feareth God and worketh righteousness is accepted by Him: Enlighten our hearts, that we may know and perceive in all nations and kindreds of people whatsoever there is in any of them that is true and honest, just and pure, lovely and of good report; through the Word that lighteth every man, Jesus Christ, our Lord. *Amen.*

261—*For the Enemies of Christ*

O GOD, the Holy Ghost, Who art come to convict the world of sin, of righteousness, and of judgment: Penetrate, we beseech Thee for Jesus' sake, the dark hard hearts of all those who have wilfully closed the door to Christ, our Lord, and let Thy light so shine upon them that they may welcome Him in His beauty; convict all enemies of the Cross, and let them see and find in Him Who died thereon the way, the truth, and the life, that where they once hated, they may love; where they sought to destroy, they may build; where they defamed, they may bear witness; Thou Who with the Father and the Son, livest and reignest, One God, world without end. *Amen.*

262—*For Our Enemies*

O CHRIST, OUR GOD, Who hast commanded us to overcome evil with good, and to pray for them who despitefully use us: Be merciful to our enemies, even as unto us, and bring them with us unto Thy heavenly Kingdom; Who with the Father and the Holy Ghost, livest and reignest, One God, world without end. *Amen.*

263—*For Our Enemies*

O LORD, Who didst command Thy disciples to love their enemies and to pray for such as despitefully used them: Mercifully grant to us to keep both these Thy words and Thine example in our hearts; and shed Thy light upon our enemies, also, that nations and men may learn the new and holy warfare of Thy love, and that we may overcome the evil in ourselves and one another with Thy good; for the glory of Thy Name and the prevalence of Thy Kingdom upon earth; Who livest and reignest with the Father and the Holy Ghost, One God, world without end. *Amen.*

264—*For the Aged*

O LORD JESUS, Whom Simeon welcomed and the aged Anna praised, and Who art the Same, yesterday, today and forever, Everlasting God: Vouchsafe unto Thy aged servants increase of spiritual might as their bodily strength faileth; and grant that as their eyes become dim and their ears dull to earthly things, their affections may be the more set on things above, and Thy peace possess their hearts and sanctify their closing days; Who with the Father and the Holy Ghost, livest and reignest, One God, world without end. *Amen.*

265—*For the Poor and Neglected*

O GOD, Almighty and Merciful, Who healest those that are broken in heart, and turnest the sadness of the sorrowful to joy; let Thy fatherly goodness be upon all that Thou hast made. Remember in pity such as are this day destitute, homeless, or forgotten of their fellowmen. Forgive us wherein we have failed to care for the sick, the helpless, and the needy, and stir us up to love and to good works. Hear us, O Lord, for the love of Him, Who for our sakes became poor, Thy Son, our Saviour, Jesus Christ. *Amen.*

266—*For the Deaf*

O LORD JESUS CHRIST, Whose compassion encompassed every infirmity of body and soul, and Who Thyself didst touch the ears of one that was deaf and opened them: Let Thy grace, we beseech Thee, rest upon all who suffer the loss of hearing; and grant that while they may not hear the sound of laughter or of music with the bodily ear, their hearts may ever know Thy loving voice, be joyous with Thy praise and be attuned to Thy Spirit; and find that harmony with Thyself which shall give them happiness in this life and joy in Thy Presence for evermore; Who livest and reignest with the Father and the Holy Spirit, ever One God, world without end. *Amen.*

267—*For the Blind*

O GOD, Who hast sent Thy Son to be the true Light of the world, grant that they who cannot see the things of the world may be the more fully enlightened and comforted by His inward guidance. Show Thyself to such as know Thee not, and quicken those who know Thee by faith to a deeper intuition of Thy love. Surround them all by such as may minister to them in sympathy and understanding, and serve Thee in serving them. And grant them such steadfast faith in this life, that in the life to come they may behold Thee as Thou art, and awake to the full revelation of Thy glory; through the Same Jesus Christ, our Lord. *Amen.*

268—*For the Mentally Sick*

O HEAVENLY FATHER, may Thy supernatural power sustain and comfort Thy servants who have lost the natural faculties of reason and selfcontrol. Suffer not the evil one to vex them, but raise up those who in wisdom and sympathy will minister to them in their need. Look upon them graciously, as redeemed by the Blood of Thy dear Son; and grant that they may be delivered from the darkness of the world, and attain to the glory of Thine immediate Presence; through the Same Jesus Christ, our Lord. *Amen.*

269—*For Prisoners*

O GOD, Who sparest when we deserve punishment, and in Thy justice art ever merciful: We humbly beseech Thee, be present with all prisoners (*esepcially those who are condemned to die*). Give them a right understanding of themselves, and of Thy promises, and work in them sorrow and true repentance for their misdeeds; that, finding forgiveness with Thee, they may place their confidence only in Thee. Relieve and comfort the distressed, succor the innocent; and as Thou alone bringest light out of darkness and good out of evil, grant to these for whom we pray, that by the power of Thy Holy Spirit they may be set free from the bondage of sin, and be brought to the glorious liberty of the children of God; through Jesus Christ, our Lord. *Amen.*

270—*For the Tempted*

O GOD, the Strength of the weak, the Friend of sinners, and the Comfort of the sorrowful: Grant Thy mighty protection to the tempted; reveal Thy grace to the fallen; maintain the faith of those who are persecuted for righteousness' sake; and give the consolation of Thy Presence to those who are disappointed, embittered, lonely, or in despair; for Thy mercy's sake in Jesus Christ, our Lord. *Amen.*

271—*In Time of Temptation*

O GOD, Who hast willed that Thy saints should be tried on earth by Thy loving probation, but not that they should be tempted above that which they are able to endure: Deliver us from the trouble which besets us, lest it overcome our mind. Aid us to serve Thee faithfully in well-pleasing obedience; and of Thy grace suffer us only to be so tried, that temptation lead us not into the confusion of error, but bind us firmly in the embrace of Thy truth; through Thy mercy, in Christ Jesus, our Lord. *Amen.*

272—*For All Those in Trouble*

O GOD, Whose Presence is everywhere and Whose mercy never faileth: Graciously regard all who are in trouble or danger, and especially those known to ourselves (*whom we now name in our hearts before Thee*); guide the wanderer, defend the innocent, restore the lost, heal the sick, comfort the bereaved, and receive the spirits of the dying; through Jesus Christ, our Lord. *Amen.*

273—*For All Those Who Need Our Prayers*

O GOD, Whose Fatherly love did ever surround Thy dear Son, Jesus: Hear us as we pray for Thy needy and suffering children:—We pray Thee for all who are handicapped by hard circumstances; for those who are being brought up in homes where there is no beauty, or joy, or love; for the sick, the incurable, the mentally deficient; for the wayward, and those who are misunderstood; for those who have lost their fathers and mothers; for those who have lost their homes; for those whose childhood has been marred by fear, and bitterness, and brutality. O God, the Father, have mercy upon them; in mercy restore that which has been taken from them; raise up fathers to the fatherless, mothers to the motherless, friends to the friendless. Wipe out from their souls the stain of misery and fear; give back to them the trustfulness and untroubled joy which should be theirs; and grant to all who care for and teach them, faith to believe that Thou art able to do all these things for them, and patient loving wisdom to co-operate with Thee; for the sake of Thy Holy Child Jesus, our Lord. *Amen.*

274—*For All Those Who Need Our Prayers—(At Eventide)*

O OUR LORD, to Whom the sick and distressed were brought at eventide to receive from Thee the healing gift of Thy loving ministry: We beseech Thee, watch Thou with those who wake, or watch, or weep this night; and give Thine angels charge over those who sleep. Tend Thy sick ones, O Christ; rest Thy weary ones; soothe and pity Thine afflicted ones; shield Thy joyous ones; and all this for Thy love's sake, Who art the Father's Love, and with Him and the Holy Spirit, livest and reignest, One God, world without end. *Amen.*

275—*A General Intercession for All Sorts and Conditions of Men*

O GOD, our Heavenly Father, we beseech Thee to hear us on behalf of all those who live by strength of arm or skill of hand; for men who face peril; for women who suffer pain; for those who till the earth; for those who tend machinery; for those whose business it is to fish in deep waters, for sailors, and for those who travel in ships; for those who work in offices, and for those who buy and sell; for those who labor at furnaces and in the factories; for those who toil in mines; for those who keep house, and for those who train children; for those who control, rule, or employ. For all whose labor is without hope, and for all whose labor is without honor; for those whose labor is without interest; for those who are underpaid, and for those who are without employment. We pray for all who have no home, for all prisoners and outcasts, for all who are sick, hungry, or destitute. We pray, O Father, for all men everywhere, that it may please Thee to comfort, sustain, protect, and support these, and all others for whom we desire to pray; through Jesus Christ, Thy Son, our Lord. *Amen.*

Hospitals, Medical Men and Nurses

HOSPITALS, MEDICAL MEN AND NURSES

276—*For Hospitals*

O LORD GOD, our Heavenly Father, compassionate and merciful, Who dost heal all our diseases and comfort us in all our distresses, and Who dost commit Thy needy and suffering children to our loving care and ministry: Be pleased to be present in this institution that it may ever be a harbor and resting-place for those troubled with sickness; and, of Thy mercy, we beseech Thee, put upon it and all that is done here to relieve and cure the distresses of body and mind, Thy healing benediction, so that thanksgivings may rise to glorify Thee, Who art our health and our song; through Jesus Christ, our Saviour. *Amen.*

277—*For a Hospital*

G RANT, O Lord Jesus Christ, to the trustees and officers of this hospital, wisdom, prudence, and grace to order and direct its affairs in accordance with Thy will. Bless the physicians and the nurses, and all members of this household, that they may duly execute their several duties in Thy fear and love, and seek only Thy honor and glory, Who didst take our infirmities and bear our sicknesses, healing all suffering humanity with Thy most precious Blood, Who now livest and reignest with the Father and the Holy Ghost, One God, world without end. *Amen.*

278—*For Those in a Hospital*

O GOD, our Father, Whose compassion never faileth; Whose love ever guardeth; Whose Presence ever aideth: Hear us, we humbly beseech Thee, when we pray for all who are here seeking health, and grant that they may find both health of body and the healing medicine of Thy saving grace; through Jesus Christ, our Lord. *Amen.*

279—*For Those in a Hospital*

O LORD JESUS CHRIST, to Whom the sick were brought that they might be healed, and Who didst send none of them away without Thy blessing: Look in pity upon all who come to Thee for healing of heart and soul and body; grant them Thy healing grace now and evermore and send them on their way, rejoicing in Thy mercy; Who with the Father and the Holy Ghost, livest and reignest, One God, world without end. *Amen.*

280—*Before Undergoing an Operation—For a Mind at Peace*

D EAR LORD, in Whom is all our hope, in Whose love is our peace now and evermore: Draw to Thee the mind of Thy servant, ... who is about to undergo an operation, and bless *him* with sure trust in Thy loving care, that finding the gift of Thy peace, *he* may know that Thou dost order all things well and wilt bless *him* as *he* hath need; Who livest and reignest with the Father and the Holy Ghost, One God, world without end. *Amen.*

281—*For Medical Men and Nurses*

O MERCIFUL FATHER, Who hast wonderfully fashioned man in Thine image, and hast made his body to be a temple of the Holy Ghost: Bless, we pray Thee, all those whom Thou hast called to study and practise the arts of healing the sick and the prevention of disease and pain; strengthen them in body and soul, and bless their work, that they themselves may live as members and servants of Christ, and give comfort to those for whom He lived and died to save; through the Same Jesus Christ, our Lord. *Amen.*

282—*For Medical Men*

O LORD, the Healer of all our diseases, Who knowest how the sick have need of a physician: Bless all whom Thou hast called to be sharers in Thine own work of healing, with health alike of body and soul: that they may learn their art in dependence upon Thee, and exercise it always under Thy sanction and to Thy glory; Who with the Father and the Holy Ghost, livest and reignest, One God, world without end. *Amen.*

283—*For the Surgeon, about to Perform an Operation*

DEAR LORD, our Great Physician, Who in Thy earthly walk didst heal the diseases of our frail bodies: Bless the surgeon, who soon shall minister to Thy servant, ..., with knowledge and skill, and guide his hand; so that all things shall work together for good, and Thy servant shall be speedily restored to health; Who livest and reignest with the Father and the Holy Ghost, One God, world without end. *Amen.*

284—*For Nurses*

O LORD JESUS CHRIST, Who hast said, Inasmuch as ye do it unto one of the least of these, my brethren, ye do it unto me: Look upon those who have been called by Thee to tend Thy sick and suffering children; give them patience and tenderness, wisdom and sympathy, and the special guidance of Thy Holy Spirit in their work, so that they may faithfully minister to those to whom Thou shalt send them; Who with the Father and the Holy Ghost, livest and reignest, One God, world without end. *Amen.*

285—*For Those Who Minister to the Sick*

O OUR FATHER, be with the nurses and all others who are about to minister to the bodily necessity of Thy servant, ..., that blessed by Thee their tender care may serve to the healing of *his* disease and an early return of health, so that we may give Thee thanks for all Thy mercy; through Jesus Christ, our Lord. *Amen.*

The City
The Nation
The World

THE CITY — THE NATION — THE WORLD

286—*National*

BLESS, we beseech Thee, Merciful Lord, our country and all its people. Give Thine abundant grace to our President, and to all who bear office throughout the land, that in all things we may be governed righteously and in Thy fear; and grant unto us, not only such outward prosperity as is according to Thy will, but, above all things, such virtue and true religion, that Thy holy Name may be ever glorified in the midst of us; through Jesus Christ, our Lord. *Amen.*

287—*National*

ALMIGHTY LORD, of Whose righteous will all things are, and were created; Who liftest the islands out of the deep, and preparest not in vain the habitable world; Thou hast gathered our people into a great nation, and sent them to sow beside all waters, and multiply sure dwellings on the earth. Deepen the root of our life in everlasting righteousness; and let not the crown of our pride be as a fading flower. Make us equal to our high trusts; reverent in the use of freedom; just in the exercise of power; generous in the protection of weakness. To our legislators and councillors give insight and faithfulness, that our laws may clearly speak the right, and our judges purely interpret them. Let it be known among us how Thou hatest robbery for burnt-offering; that the gains of industry may be all upright, and the use of wealth considerate. May wisdom and knowledge be the stability of our times: and our deepest trust be in Thee, the Lord of nations and the King of kings; through Jesus Christ, our Lord. *Amen.*

288—*For Our Native Land*

O GOD, Who hast ever been gracious to our nation; Who in former times, even from the midst of trouble, hast led us through to days of peace: Make of us a people worthy of Thy gracious protection; ward from us every evil which may arise to harm us; preserve us from every enemy within and without; and in Thy mercy, help us so to build upon the foundations laid by our fathers so surely in Thee, that we may ever know and seek those things which belong unto our peace and be indeed a Christian nation to the praise of Thy Name and the good of all mankind; through Him Who is our Peace, even Jesus Christ, Thy Son, our Lord. *Amen.*

289—*Washington's Prayer for the United States of America*

ALMIGHTY GOD: We make our earnest prayer that Thou wilt keep the United States in Thy holy protection; that Thou wilt incline the hearts of the citizens to cultivate a spirit of subordination and obedience to government, and entertain a brotherly affection and love for one another and for their fellow citizens of the United States at large. And finally that Thou wilt most graciously be pleased to dispose us all to do justice, to love mercy, and demean ourselves with that charity, humility and pacific temper of mind which were the characteristics of the Divine Author of our blessed religion, without a humble imitation of Whose example in these things we can never hope to be a happy nation. Grant our supplication, we beseech Thee, through Jesus Christ, our Lord. *Amen.*

290—*For the Spirit of Loyal Service*

QUICKEN, O Lord God, in all the land the spirit of loyal service; that old and young, remembering this day those who have given their lives for their country, may be inspired by their sacrifice to serve our people and nation unselfishly, promote righteousness and strive for the peace and welfare of all mankind; through Jesus Christ, our Lord. *Amen.*

291—*National*

ALMIGHTY GOD, our Heavenly Father, bless our country that it may be a blessing to the world; grant that our ideals and aspirations may be in accordance with Thy will, and help us to see ourselves as others see us. Keep us from hypocrisy in feeling or action. Grant us sound government and just laws, good education, and a clean press, simplicity and justice in our relations with one another, and, above all, a spirit of service which will abolish pride of place and inequality of opportunity; through Jesus Christ, our Lord. *Amen.*

292—*For the Men of the Land*

O LORD JESUS CHRIST, Who art very God and very Man: Grant, we pray Thee, to the Christian men of this land grace to withstand the temptations of the world, the flesh, and the devil; graft in their hearts love of Thy Name; increase in them true religion; make them zealous and faithful soldiers of the Cross and a bulwark of the Church and the nation, to the praise and glory of Thy holy Name; Who livest and reignest with the Father and the Holy Ghost, One God, world without end. *Amen.*

293—*For the Women of the Land*

O LORD JESUS CHRIST, Who in Thy tender love and great humility didst come down from heaven to be born of a woman: Make, we pray Thee, the Christian women of this land, after the example of Thy blessed Mother, pure and strong in spirit, modest and gentle in conduct, truthful, unselfish, and obedient to Thy holy will; that radiant with Thy love, they may ever serve and praise Thee; Who livest and reignest with the Father and the Holy Ghost, One God, world without end. *Amen.*

294—*For the Youth of the Land*

O LORD JESUS CHRIST, grant that the young people of our country may live before Thee in purity, always remembering that they are Thy members, and using the strength of their bodies according to the energy of Thy holiness for Thy glory, Who art the Source of their life and the Captain of their salvation. Reveal Thyself in their hearts, we pray, that being filled with Thy wisdom, they may know Thee as the Pattern of meekness and purity, of diligence and obedience, of endurance and hope; and rising above all earthly passion, they may live in the light of Thy truth and ever follow Thee; Who with the Father and the Holy Ghost, livest and reignest, One God, world without end. *Amen.*

295—*For Those Who Come from Other Lands*

O GOD, Who hast commanded us to welcome the stranger within our gates: We humbly entreat Thee for those who enter our land seeking the opportunities of life with which Thou hast blest our nation; that, in Thy mercy, they may learn to know and treasure the ideals and freedom which are our precious heritage; and, ordering their lives in accordance with Thy holy Word, may become good and loyal citizens of our country, so that they with us, and we with them may dwell together in mutual understanding and helpfulness as one united people joyfully serving Thee; through Jesus Christ, our Lord. *Amen.*

296—*For Our People*

O LORD JESUS CHRIST, Who by Thy Apostle hast commanded us to pray for all men: In mercy regard this our people in all their many and varied walks and occupations, and enlighten all hearts with the glory of Thy Gospel, so that we may not live for ourselves and for those things which are passing, but obeying the law of Thy life, may live for Thee and for each other; Who with the Father and the Holy Ghost, livest and reignest, One God, world without end. *Amen.*

297—*For the National Government*

O GOD, Whose alone is the Kingdom, and the Power and the Glory, yet Who hast ordained human government for the temporal welfare of mankind: Grant and continue unto us a succession of legislators and executives who have been taught the wisdom of the Kingdom of Christ. Endow all members of Government with a right understanding, a pure purpose and sound speech; enable them to rise above all self-seeking and party zeal into the larger sentiments of public good and human brotherhood. Purge our political life of every evil; make us to love peace and fair-dealing. Inspire us with calmness and self-restraint and the endeavor to further the doing of Thy will everywhere upon the earth; through Jesus Christ, our Lord. *Amen.*

298—*A Prayer by Luther for Good Government*

LORD, preserve Thy people; maintain true, righteous justice and worldly government everywhere; so that all things may take place in an orderly way and peace may not be destroyed by revolution or secret enmity and plotting, nor the external good order be corrupted by debased and impure living or disturbed by other offenses. *Amen.*

299—*For the Nation and the President*

BLESS we beseech Thee, merciful Lord, our country and all our people. Give Thine especial aid and grace to the President of the United States. Be his Counsellor and his Defense. Give him faith, wisdom, courage, health and patience to bear the burden of his office. Keep him in safety and grant that, relying upon Thee and seeking to do Thy will, he and his associates in government may enact wise laws and administer them justly, so that the welfare of our people may be assured and peace maintained at home and among the nations of the world; through Jesus Christ, Thy Son, our Lord. *Amen.*

300—*For Congress*

O GOD MOST HIGH, Who alone rulest in the kingdom of men: Grant, we beseech Thee, to all members of Congress (*or, the Legislature*) the inspiration of Thy Holy Spirit, that they may labor faithfully for the welfare of our nation and the people and for the advancement of Thy Kingdom upon earth; through Jesus Christ, our Lord. *Amen.*

301—*Local Government*

O FATHER of the just, do Thou of Thine infinite goodness direct the hearts of all who bear authority. Help them with the power of Thy Holy Spirit to make laws in accordance with Thy will, and for the advancement of righteousness. Protect them from the snares of the enemy and the deceits of the world; let no pride of power betray them into rejection of Thy commandments; and grant that all our executives and officials and our whole people may with one mind serve Thee, our God and King; through Jesus Christ, our Lord. *Amen.*

302—*For Our City*

O GOD, grant us a vision of our city, fair as she might be; a city of justice, where none shall prey on others; a city of plenty, where vice and poverty shall cease to fester; a city of brotherhood, where all success shall be founded on service, and honor shall be given to nobleness alone; a city of peace, where order shall not rest on force, but on the love of all for the city, the great mother of the common life and weal. Hear Thou, O Lord, the silent prayer of all our hearts as we each pledge our time and strength and thought to speed the day of her coming beauty and righteousness; through Jesus Christ, our Lord. *Amen.*

303—*For Our City or Community*

GRANT, Lord, that we may love our city (*community*) with a holy love, being turned aside by no wickedness in high or low places, but with steadfastness of purpose and unremitting zeal, labor together with all who love righteousness, to purify and cleanse, to enlighten and inspire; that our city (*community*) may do justly, love kindness and walk humbly with Thee, our God; through Jesus Christ, our Lord. *Amen.*

304—*Before an Election*

ALMIGHTY GOD, the Fountain of all wisdom: Guide and direct, we humbly beseech Thee, the minds of all those who are called at this time to elect fit persons to serve in the government of this nation (*or, the government of this county, or, city, or, town, or, place*); grant that in the exercise of their choice they may promote Thy glory and the welfare of Thy people; and to those who shall be elected give, we pray Thee, the spirit of wisdom and true godliness. All this we beg for the sake of our Lord and Saviour, Jesus Christ. *Amen.*

305—*Before a National Election*

O LORD, we beseech Thee to govern the minds of all who are called at this time to choose faithful men for the governing of our nation; that they may exercise their choice as in Thy sight, for the welfare of all our people; through Jesus Christ, our Lord. *Amen.*

306—*For the Armed Forces of the Nation*

ALMIGHTY and Everlasting God, Whose Providence hath given unto us as a people this great land stored with treasure and around it hath cast like a mantle the sea: Bless we pray Thee, the officers and men of our Army, our Navy, and our Air Forces, as they perform the duties of their calling: give them not only true love of country, but also love of Thee, and understanding of Thy love for all mankind; so that, relying upon Thine almighty aid, they may courageously defend our nation from every foe, promote righteousness, honor and unity among our people in times of peace, and be a means of fostering mutual respect and understanding among the peoples of the world; through Jesus Christ, Thy Son, our Lord. *Amen.*

307—*The Army* (*For Use of Chaplains*)

O LORD GOD OF HOSTS, stretch forth the shield of Thy mighty protection over us Thy servants, and over the Army (*or, Regiment*) in which we serve. Lead and guide us evermore by the counsel of Thy goodness; strengthen us with Thy might; that we may steadfastly continue an honor and bulwark of our land, a sure defense against every enemy, and an instrument of service for the good of all; through Jesus Christ, our Lord. *Amen.*

308—*The Navy* (*For Use of Chaplains*)

O ETERNAL LORD GOD, Who alone spreadest out the heavens and rulest the raging of the sea, and hast compassed the waters with bounds until day and night come to an end: Be pleased to receive into Thy almighty and most gracious protection the persons of us, Thy servants, and the fleet (*or, ship*) in which we serve. Preserve us from the dangers of the deep and from the violence of enemies, and enable us to do the duty that may fall to us; that for the inhabitants of our land and for all mankind there may be peace and freedom to serve Thee; and that in due season we may return to our homes, with a thankful remembrance of Thy mercies; through Jesus Christ, our Lord. *Amen.*

309—*For a World in Confusion*

O SPIRIT OF GOD, Who didst move upon the face of the waters and didst bring order out of chaos and light out of darkness: Brood over the world filled with strife and bitterness and unholy rivalries; calm the passions of men, quiet their fears; and breathe into them the spirit of forgiveness and of loving service, that peace and goodwill may prevail in the earth. Be merciful to those who have been driven from their homes by oppression, to widows and orphans, to those who are friendless, alone in the world. Comfort them in their distress; raise up friends and helpers for them from among those who have plenty; and may their faith in Thee not fail. O God, be merciful unto us; grant peace in our time; this we ask in the Name of Jesus Christ, our Lord. *Amen.*

310—*For the Troubled World*

O GOD, at Whose Word chaos became an ordered creation: Brood over this troubled world, as once Thy Spirit brooded o'er the face of the deep, and create in the nations, by the grace of Thy Son, that love for Thee and for each other, which will make this world a new creation in righteousness and peace and joy, in brotherhood and mutual service; through the saving merit of the Same Thy Son, Jesus Christ, our Lord. *Amen.*

311—*For the Tranquillity of the World*

ALMIGHTY GOD, Who art the true Joy of every man and nation that serveth Thee: We humbly pray, Thy Kingdom come; so that Thy truth and justice may abide in all the nations of the world and all the peoples may delight to make Thy holy will their daily law; through Jesus Christ, our Lord. *Amen.*

312—*For World Peace*

O GOD, the Father in Heaven, grant Thy mighty aid to the efforts of men to establish peace among the nations of the world. Give strength of purpose to those who lead; enlighten those who sit in council; and so transform the hearts of men everywhere by Thy gracious Gospel, that they may exalt peace above war, service above gain, and righteousness above glory; through Jesus Christ, our Lord. *Amen.*

313—*International Accord*

O ALMIGHTY GOD, the Refuge of all them that put their trust in Thee: Direct the course of this world, we humbly beseech Thee, in accordance with Thy holy will; take away whatsoever hinders the nations from attaining unity and concord; prosper all counsels which make for rightful peace; this we ask for Thy mercy's sake, through Jesus Christ, our Lord. *Amen.*

314—*For True Nationalism (For the Nations of the World)*

LORD GOD ALMIGHTY, Father of mankind and Ruler of nations: Raise up, we beseech Thee, true prophets and leaders in every land, who, discerning the peculiar gifts and tasks which Thou hast given to the nations severally, may, without fear or flattery, teach their people the way that they should go; that the nations of the world, guided by Thy providence, may fulfil their appointed destinies and minister under Thee to the enrichment and happiness of the life of mankind; through Jesus Christ, our Lord. *Amen.*

315—*In Time of War*

O LORD GOD of infinite mercy, we humbly beseech Thee to look down upon the nations now engaged in war. Reckon not against Thy people their many iniquities, but grant them true repentance and amendment of life that the lust of man's heart may be conquered by Thy Spirit of gentleness and righteousness. Look in mercy on those immediately exposed to peril, conflict, sickness, and death: comfort the prisoners, relieve the sufferings of the wounded, and show mercy to the dying. Remove in Thy good providence all causes and occasions of war; dispose the hearts of those engaged therein to moderation; and of Thy great goodness restore peace among the nations; through Jesus Christ, our Lord. *Amen.*

316—*In Time of War*

FATHER of mercies and God of all comfort, Who in all our affliction art afflicted; look in pity upon all who are suffering in this time of strife and warfare of nations. Protect the defenseless, succor the wounded, receive the dying, and console the anxious and bereaved. Turn the hearts of our enemies, we beseech Thee, and forgive both them and us for our share in the sin that has brought this anguish on mankind; open up to us a way of reconciliation and lead us into the path of peace; through Jesus Christ, our only Redeemer. *Amen.*

317—*Memorial Days*

WE praise and bless Thy glorious Name, O Lord, for the devoted sacrifice of Thy servants who have laid down their lives that we might live. Into Thy holy keeping we commend their souls, and humbly pray, that we, like they, may give and never count the cost, fight and never heed the wounds, toil and never seek for rest, labor and ask for no reward save the knowledge that we do Thy will; through Jesus Christ, our Lord. *Amen.*

318—*Memorial Days*

O GOD, our Heavenly Father, we thank Thee for all who have laid down their lives for home, and country, and for righteousness; and especially for Thy *servants,* whom we remember before Thee this day; and we pray Thee, that all, who have fought the good fight, may receive from Thee the crown of everlasting life; through Jesus Christ, our Lord. *Amen.*

319—*Public and Other Holidays*

DEAR LORD, Who didst look with joy upon the beauties of wayside and field; Who didst take Thy little company away to quiet places for refreshment and rest: We thank Thee for the seasons of refreshment and recreation which come amid the strains and cares of our daily life and employment; and beseech Thee that we may so appreciate their value to both spirit and body, that we may use them to our profit and to the renewal of strength and will for the doing of our appointed tasks faithfully. *Amen.*

Times and Seasons

TIMES AND SEASONS

320—*Morning*

WE give thanks unto Thee, Heavenly Father, through Jesus Christ, Thy dear Son, that Thou hast protected us through the night from all danger and harm; and we beseech Thee to preserve and keep us, this day also, from all sin and evil; that in all our thoughts, words and deeds, we may serve and please Thee. Into Thy hands we commend our bodies and souls, and all that is ours. Let Thy holy angel have charge concerning us, that the wicked one have no power over us. *Amen.*

321—*Morning*

WE give Thee thanks, Almighty God, that Thou hast delivered us from the darkness of the night, and dost now shine on us with the light of day: Pour into our hearts, the pure and serene light of Thy truth, that we may avoid the darkness of sin, and ever know and follow Thee, the eternal light; through Jesus Christ, our Lord. *Amen.*

322—*Morning*

O LORD, give Thy blessing, we pray Thee, to our daily work, that we may do it in faith and heartily, as to the Lord and not unto men. All our powers of body and mind are Thine, and we would earnestly devote them to Thy service. Sanctify them, and the work in which they are engaged; let us not be slothful, but fervent in spirit; and do Thou, O Lord, so bless our efforts that they may bring forth in us the fruits of true wisdom. Give us this day our daily bread, that we may be nourished in our body. Give us this day Thy Holy Spirit, that we may be nourished in our soul. Give us this day opportunity for service, that we may live to Thy praise; through Jesus Christ, our Lord. *Amen.*

323—*For Sunday Morning*

AS the hart panteth after the water-brooks, O God, our souls do thirst after Thee, that we may see Thy power and Thy glory, as we have seen them in the sanctuary, and be satisfied with the goodness of Thy house. Lead us and guide us unto Thy holy hill, and bring us together with sweet converse to the place of prayer, to hear Thy Word of truth in the spirit, to offer the sacrifices of joy with Thy people, and to make melody in our hearts with the songs of Zion. Prepare us, we beseech Thee, for a true entrance into the secret of Thy tabernacle; and bless Thy churches everywhere this day with the beauty of Thy Presence; that the Holy Spirit may descend on many hearts, and multitudes may be brought from the kingdom of evil into the Kingdom of Thy dear Son, Jesus Christ. *Amen.*

324—*At the Beginning of a New Day*

O GOD, of Whose gift is the brilliance of a golden morn: Enlighten my (*our*) heart with the radiance of Thy love, that in its beauty I (*we*) may praise Thee and shine with the gladness of righteousness and the gentleness of peace all the day long; through Him, Who is the Sun of righteousness and the Splendor of Thy glory, Jesus Christ, our Lord. *Amen.*

325—*Evening*

INTO Thy hands we commit ourselves, Blessed Lord, this night and forever. O Thou Sun of righteousness, keep us from utter darkness; and let us so sleep in peace that we may be ready at all times to arise and meet Thee, when Thou comest in Thy glory, Who, with the Father and the Holy Ghost, art One God, world without end. *Amen.*

326—*Evening*

O LORD, support us all the day long of this troublous life, until the shadows lengthen, and the evening comes, and the busy world is hushed, and the fever of life is over, and our work is done; then, O Lord, in Thy mercy, grant us safe lodging, a holy rest, and peace at the last; through Jesus Christ, our Lord. *Amen.*

327—*Evening*

WE give thanks unto Thee, Heavenly Father, through Jesus Christ, Thy dear Son, that Thou hast this day so graciously protected us, and we beseech Thee to forgive us all our sins, and the wrong which we have done, and by Thy great mercy defend us from all the perils and dangers of this night. Into Thy hands we commend our bodies and souls, and all that is ours. Let Thy holy angel have charge concerning us, that the wicked one have no power over us. *Amen.*

328—*Evening*

WATCH over us, O Lord, Heavenly Father, and preserve us from every evil which may happen to the body and soul. Grant us grace to take our rest this night in safety beneath Thy protection. Guard and bless Thy Church and this Thy congregation. Graciously remember, in Thy mercy, those who are in sickness, in need, and in peril. Have mercy upon all mankind; and when at length our last evening cometh grant us then to fall asleep in Thy peace, that we may awake in Thy glory; through Jesus Christ, our Lord. *Amen.*

329—*Evening*

BLESSED art Thou Who hast granted us to pass through this day and to reach the beginning of the night. Hear our prayers and those of all Thy people. Forgive us our sins and accept our evening supplications. Send down on Thine inheritance the fullness of Thy mercy. Arm us with the armor of Thy righteousness, fence us round with Thy truth, guard us with Thy power. Deliver us from every assault and device of evil; and grant us to pass this evening, and the approaching night, and all the days of our life, in fullness of peace and holiness; through Jesus Christ, our Lord. *Amen.*

330—*For the Morrow*

ABIDE with us, Lord God of Hosts, and, when in the morning we shall rise from the rest of Thy gracious gift this night, take heed unto us, and guide all our acts, words, and thoughts, that we may pass through the coming day in accordance with Thy will. Set a watch over our eyes lest they behold vanity. Set a watch about our ears that they listen not to falsehood and folly, but may always be ready to attend to Thy Word. Set a watch over our hands that they may do no wrong, but may ever in peace and purity be lifted up in prayer to Thee. Set a watch over our lips that we may utter no vain words, neither slandering those that are absent, nor speaking evil of those that are present, nor rendering unto any railing for railing; but that we may bless Thee at all times, and that Thy praise may always be in our mouths; through Jesus Christ, our Saviour. *Amen.*

331—*Spring*

O EVERLASTING GOD, Who art the eternal Fountain and only Giver of life: We bless Thee that we may again behold on every side the awakening of nature in answer to Thy call to arise from winter's sleep; and as Thou dost cheer our spirits with the freshening grass and budding trees and unfolding plants, grant us thankful hearts to praise Thee for the promise of Thy renewed provision for our body and life and an abiding trust in Thy unchanging love now and eternally; through Jesus Christ, Thy Son, our Lord. *Amen.*

332—*Summer*

O OUR FATHER, Who through Thy dear Son dost bid us consider the lilies of the field that we may know the sureness of Thy fatherly provision and behold the glory of Thy handiwork even in the wayside flower: We bless Thee for the joy and beauty of the summer days, for abounding life, for glad nature all around, for warmth and light, for promise of fruitage, for hours of enjoyment and refreshment; as Thou dost shower upon us these Thy blessings, so may we rejoice to pour forth our praises to Thee, and use Thy bounties with thankful and sharing hearts; through Jesus Christ, Thy Son, our Lord. *Amen.*

333—*Autumn*

O ALMIGHTY GOD, Whose glory the heavens declare: Open our eyes to behold and our hearts to praise Thee for Thy handiwork revealed in the harvested fields, and in forests and hills, clothed with beauty and color; and as we rejoice anew in Thy good providence and thankfully store up the fruits of the earth for our nourishment, let the gladness and praise of our hearts clothe us with the beauty of faith and trust, which shall witness before all men to Thy glory; through Jesus Christ, Thy Son, our Lord. *Amen.*

334—*Winter*

O ALMIGHTY GOD, Whose years know neither beginning nor end; Who hast cheered and refreshed us with the return of spring, nourished us with summer days, enriched us with the bounty and beauty of autumn: We praise Thy providence which blesses the labors of nature with winter's rest, and which will call it to awaken again to serve Thy will; and we beseech Thee to grant us faith to trust our life to Thy direction, knowing that Thou dost order all things for our present and eternal good, sealing the labors of this present life in the peace and joy of life unending; through Jesus Christ, Thy Son, our Lord. *Amen.*

335—*Seed-time*

O ALMIGHTY GOD, our Heavenly Father, Who dost minister seed to the sower and bread to the eater: Nourish, protect, and bless the seed which men are now sowing in hope; so that by Thy good ordering and bounteous giving, it may bring forth fruit in due season, and be harvested with thanksgiving to satisfy the desires of Thy people with nourishing food; through Jesus Christ, Thy Son, our Lord. *Amen.*

336—*Growing-time*

O LORD GOD, our Father, by Whose loving provision the wide reaches of the earth bring forth food for man and beast: Withhold not, we beseech Thee, Thy open and sustaining hand, but bless the fields and farms, the hills and vales, the trees and grass, that nature may bring forth her fruits in due season, and men may take of Thy gifts for themselves and for the humble beasts which serve them; through Jesus Christ, Thy Son, our Lord. *Amen.*

337—*Harvest-time*

O LORD JESUS CHRIST, Almighty and Gracious, Who didst reveal Thy almighty power and loving heart in word and deed when Thou didst satisfy the hungry thousands with a few small loaves: We thank Thee for Thy fatherly provision and care; for our daily bread and the nourishing fruits of the earth; and for all the good things with which Thou dost bless us; and we beseech Thee, grant us grace to treasure these blessings of Thy gracious heart and bounteous hand, using them with thankfulness and care, so that we may serve our children and the needs of the poor with Thy gifts, and ever thank and praise Thee, the Giver of all good, Who with the Father and the Holy Ghost, livest and reignest, One God, world without end. *Amen.*

338—*For Rain*

O GOD, our Heavenly Father, Who by Thy gracious providence dost cause the early and the later rain to fall upon the earth: Send us at the last in this our necessity, we beseech Thee, a blessing rain; that the parched ground may be refreshed and there be water both for man and beast, to the great comfort of us Thy unworthy servants and to the glory of Thy holy Name; and this we beg for our Lord, Jesus Christ's sake. *Amen.*

339—*For Good Weather*

O GOD, by Whose good providence alone we receive the fruits of the earth in due season: We beseech Thee of Thy mercy to send us such weather, that our fields may bring forth abundantly; so that in the time of harvest we may give Thee thanks with gladness and joyfulness of heart; through Jesus Christ, Thy Son, our Lord. *Amen.*

340—*Thanksgiving*

O MERCIFUL GOD, at Whose bidding the earth withholdeth her increase, or again rendereth her fruits in their season: Give us grace that we may learn, alike from Thy mercies and from Thy judgments, our entire dependence on Thee for the supply of our daily bread; and, being fully persuaded that whatever blessing we receive at Thy hands is designed for our trial, as well as for our comfort, may we give Thee of that which is Thine own, by contributing to the maintenance of Thy holy Church, and the relief of the poor and the afflicted, the widow and the orphan; to the glory of Thy Name, through Jesus Christ, our Lord. *Amen.*

341—*Thanksgiving*

O ALMIGHTY GOD and Heavenly Father, we glorify Thee that Thou hast again fulfilled to us Thy gracious promise, that while the earth remaineth seedtime and harvest shall not fail. We bless Thee for the kindly fruits of the earth, which Thou hast given to our use. Teach us, we beseech Thee, to remember that it is not by bread alone that man doth live, and grant us evermore to feed on Him Who is the true Bread from heaven, even Jesus Christ our Lord, to Whom, with Thee and the Holy Ghost, be all honor and glory, world without end. *Amen.*

342—*Thanksgiving*

O ALMIGHTY and Everlasting God, Who hast given unto us the fruits of the earth in their season: We thank Thee for all these Thy blessings which Thou hast provided for the nourishment of our bodies; and we pray Thee to grant us grace ever to use the same to Thy glory, to the relief of those who are needy, and, thankfully, to our own comfort; through Jesus Christ, our Lord. *Amen.*

The Church Year

THE CHURCH YEAR

343—*Advent*

O LORD GOD, Heavenly Father, Who hast revealed to us through Thy Son how heaven and earth shall pass away: We beseech Thee keep us steadfast in Thy Word and in true faith; graciously guard us from all sin and preserve us amid all temptations, so that our hearts may not be overcharged with the cares of this life, but at all times in watchfulness and prayer may await the return of Thy Son and the expectation of our eternal salvation with joy; through the Same Thy Son, Jesus Christ, our Lord. *Amen.*

344—*Advent*

A LMIGHTY FATHER, by the advent of Whose Son into the world the Kingdom of Heaven is open to all who believe in Him: Grant us Thy Holy Spirit so that we may believe in Him with our whole heart, and so serve Him in our daily lives that when He cometh again to make up His jewels, we may, by Thy mercy be gathered into the Kingdom which abideth eternal in the heavens; through Thy mercy, O our God, Who livest and reignest One God, world without end. *Amen.*

345—*Advent*

O LORD JESUS CHRIST, Who at Thy first coming didst send Thy messenger to prepare Thy way before Thee: Grant that the ministers and stewards of Thy mysteries may likewise so prepare and make ready Thy way, by turning the hearts of the disobedient to the wisdom of the just, that at Thy second coming to judge the world we may be found an acceptable people in Thy sight, Who livest and reignest with the Father and the Holy Ghost, ever One God, world without end. *Amen.*

346—*Advent*

O JESUS, Sun of Righteousness, rise in our hearts and enlighten us with the brightness of Thy coming, that we, who rejoice in the sure word of Thy promise, may not be confounded at Thy coming in glory; through Thy mercy, O our God, Who with the Father and the Holy Ghost, livest and dost govern all things now and evermore. *Amen.*

347—*Advent*

O LORD, make us to live soberly, justly, and righteously in this present age; and, as we look for that blessed hope and the coming of Thy glory, may we walk in the path of holiness that, by Thy grace, we may come to the eternal inheritance which Thou hast prepared for those who love Thee; through Thy mercy, O our God, Who art blessed for evermore. *Amen.*

348—*Advent*

G RANT, O Almighty God, that as Thy blessed Son, Jesus Christ, at His first advent came to seek and to save that which was lost, so at His second and glorious appearing He may find in us the fruits of the redemption which He wrought; through the Same Jesus Christ, our Lord. *Amen.*

349—*Holy Night*

O LORD JESUS CHRIST, Who by Thy incarnation didst unite things earthly and things heavenly: Fill us with the sweetness of inward peace and good will, and grant us to be companions of the heavenly host in raising praises to Thy glory; Who livest and reignest with the Father and the Holy Ghost, One God, world without end. *Amen.*

350—*Holy Night*

G LORY be to Thee at all times, Almighty Lord, Jesus Christ, the confession of Whose praise filleth heaven and earth: While glory is sung to Thee in the highest and on earth peace is announced to men, grant, we beseech

Thee, good will to us Thy servants, so that Thou mayest cleanse us from all sins and graciously bestow Thine abiding peace upon us and all people, Who with the Father and the Holy Ghost, livest and reignest, One God, now and evermore. *Amen.*

351—*Christmas*

O GOD, our Heavenly Father, Who dost call to our remembrance the birthday of Thy Son, our Saviour Jesus Christ: Give us grace to keep this festival with pure faith and holy love; that while we join our voices with theirs who sang glory to God in the highest, we may not forget to spread abroad also the gospel of Thy peace and good will towards men; through the Same, Thy Son, Jesus Christ, our Lord. *Amen.*

352—*Christmas*

OUR FATHER, of Whose love the angels sang when Jesus was born in Bethlehem, and through Whom we have learned the song of praise, Glory be to Thee in the highest: Accept our worship and our hymns of joy; and, as we celebrate the birthday of Thy Son, grant that in Him we may learn to know Thy love, to follow Him in obedience, and to offer ourselves to Thee in all things, that our lives may show us, too, to be Thy children in all our thoughts, words, and deeds; through the Same Jesus Christ, Thy Son, our Lord. *Amen.*

353—*Christmas*

O LORD JESUS CHRIST, Who in Thy incarnation didst visit this world with Thy Presence, and Whose coming again to judgment every believing soul expects: Be gracious unto us and justify us in the day of Thy coming with Thy divine mercy, that we, who now celebrate the festival of Thy incarnation, may then be joined to the company of Thy saints; Who with the Father and the Holy Ghost, livest and reignest, One God, world without end. *Amen.*

354—*Christmas*

O GOD, Who hast given us grace at this time to celebrate the birth of our Saviour, Jesus Christ: We laud and magnify Thy glorious Name for the countless blessings which He hath brought unto us; and we beseech Thee to grant that we may ever set forth Thy praise in joyful obedience to Thy will; through the Same Jesus Christ, our Lord. *Amen.*

355—*New Year's Day*

O LORD GOD, Almighty Creator, from Whom cometh every good and perfect gift; Who hast blessed us so bountifully during the year past, in that Thou hast preserved unto us Thy Word, kept us in Thy care and in peace, provided for our bodily needs, and protected our state, our schools, our church, and those near and dear unto us: We thank and praise Thee for all Thy goodness to us, and beseech Thee, in Thy mercy grant us a blessed new year; graciously maintain and prosper Thy Word and all good discipline, keeping us and our government in continued peace; and aid us to grow in faith, love, patience and to submit to all lawful authority; let Thy fatherly protection be over our dear ones and us; and of Thy mercy speedily bring the coming of the new and eternal year of jubilee; through Jesus Christ the new-born Babe, our eternal King and Lord. *Amen.*

356—*New Year*

O GOD, Who art ever the Same: Grant us to pass through the coming year with faithful hearts, that we may be able in all things to please Thy loving eyes; through Jesus Christ, our Lord. *Amen.*

357—*New Year*

O GOD, Who art ever the Same, and Whose years know no end: In Thy mercy we close another year of time, and lay it away in Thy eternal storehouse. It has been filled with Thy goodness toward us: for this we humbly thank

Thee. It has known our sins, and disobedience, and failures: for these we grieve and beseech Thy forgiveness. It has seen our feeble efforts in service of Thee and our fellow-men: purify this all and find, we humbly pray, something therein which may be to Thy glory. Grant us Thy grace so to enter this new year that we may count every day a new privilege of life and opportunity to learn of Thee, that through us Thy Name may be hallowed, in us Thy King-dom come, and by us Thy will be done; through Jesus Christ, Thy Son, our Lord. *Amen.*

358—*New Year*

ALMIGHTY GOD, have mercy upon us, who, when troubled with the things that are past, lose faith, and courage, and hope. In Thy grace uphold us, that we, being sustained by a true faith that Thou art merciful and forgiv-ing, may go forward; keep Thy commandments; rejoice in Thy bounty; trust in Thy mercy; and hope for eternal life. Grant that whate'er betide we may always remember that we are in Thy keeping, so that, in darkest days, close to Thee, we may have courage to go on and faith to endure, even unto the end; through Jesus Christ, our Lord. *Amen.*

359—*Epiphany*

O GOD, our Heavenly Father, Whose guiding star led the wise men to our Lord's manger through a long, perilous, and unknown way: We pray Thee Who hast made Thy Son our way through life, to keep us steadfast in following Him, to guide us and ever teach us by His ex-ample, to protect and counsel us by His Spirit; so that we may come safely to our heavenly home where all Thy children will ever adore Thee, the Father of love, through Jesus Christ, Thy Son, in Thy Holy Spirit. *Amen.*

360—*Epiphany*

O LORD GOD, Heavenly Father, Who hast made Thy precious Word, the true star which leadeth to Thy Child Jesus, to shine for us: We beseech Thee, shed Thy Holy Spirit into our hearts, so that we may receive this light with joy and thanksgiving and use the same for our salvation; that like the wise men, we may follow that star, permit no hardship or danger to affright or deter us; and, accepting Thy Son as our only Saviour, offer of those gifts which Thou hast given us for our life's need, to the maintenance and spread of Thy Christendom here on earth, so that Thy Name may be glorified; through the Same, Thy Son, Jesus Christ, our Lord. *Amen.*

361—*Epiphany*

A LMIGHTY GOD, Who at the baptism of Thy blessed Son Jesus Christ in the river Jordan didst manifest His glorious Godhead: Grant, we beseech Thee, that the brightness of His Presence may shine in our hearts, and His glory be set forth in our lives; through the Same Jesus Christ, our Lord. *Amen.*

362—*Epiphany* (*For the Church*) (*IV Sunday*)

O ALMIGHTY SON OF GOD, Who art our sole Protector and Help in time of need: Behold Thy little bark, the Church, suffereth great need, for the winds of evil blow against it, the sea of world rebellion rageth, the waves of man's wrong and sin dash over us and seek to engulf us: if Thou forsake us, Lord, we perish. Therefore, arise, O Master, and rebuke the angry tempests and bless us with Thy peace; for all our enemies are held in the hollow of Thy hand, O Thou, Who ever watchest and guarded us, and dost abide with us in Thy ship now and evermore. *Amen.*

363—*Transfiguration*

O GOD, Who allowest us to celebrate the day of Thy transfiguration with devout praises: Grant us, we beseech Thee, to attain the vision of Thy divinity, Who didst deign to become partaker of our humanity: Who, with the Father and the Holy Ghost, livest and reignest, One God, world without end. *Amen.*

364—*The Transfiguration of Life*

O LORD JESUS CHRIST, Who didst take Thy loved disciples with Thee on the mount of transfiguration: We beseech Thee find for us quiet hours in this busy life, and there commune with us and teach us; so that we may be transfigured by Thy grace, filled with Thy truth and adore Thy glory, which Thou revealest to those who abide in Thee. *Amen.*

365—*Lent*

LET Thy blessing be upon us, Heavenly Father, as we pass through these holy days in which we remember the sufferings and death of our dear Lord; and grant that His holy example being ever before us, we may follow Him in willing obedience, learn His gracious humility, and, being filled with His love and spirit of self-sacrifice, learn the lessons of a life pleasing to Thee and helpful to our fellowmen; through Him Who loved us and gave Himself for us, even Jesus Christ, our Lord. *Amen.*

366—*Lent*

O GRACIOUS FATHER, Whose dearly loved Son has taught us that whosoever will be His disciple must take up his cross and follow Him: Help us so to follow our Lord through these days in which we commemorate His bitter sufferings and passion that as He, for the joy that was set before Him, endured the shame and Cross, so we may learn of Him, by His grace, to be faithful in all things; through the Same, Thy Son, Jesus Christ, our Lord. *Amen.*

367—*Lent*

WE entreat Thee, O Lord our God, with our whole
heart, forgive our sins and correct our misdeeds;
direct our actions and inspire us with thoughts well pleasing to Thee; purify our consciences and sanctify our hearts,
subduing the flesh to the spirit, and the spirit to Thyself;
so that, in purity of heart and gladness of spirit we may
serve Thee, our Lord and God; through Jesus Christ, our
Lord. *Amen.*

368—*Lent* (*Reminiscere*)

O GOD, our Father, Who dost graciously hear all who
call on Thee, Whose providence directeth Thy saints,
Who in Thine own good time savest us, even though Thy
help seemeth for a time to be withheld: Graciously open
Thy ears to our petition and lead us by Thy Spirit, that
without doubting we may persevere in prayer and be-
lievingly await Thy promised help; through Jesus Christ,
our Lord. *Amen.*

369—*Lent*

HEAVENLY FATHER, Who didst send Thy Son to sinful men, and didst lay on Him the grievous burden
of the Cross, that we might see and know the glory of Thy
holy love: Grant that our faith in Him may not be shaken
by adversity or daunted by the threat of it, but that we may
ever follow steadfastly the way that leads to perfect fellowship with Him, and so with Thee; through the Same Jesus
Christ, our Lord. *Amen.*

370—*Lent*

O GOD, Who givest strength to the weak and light to
those who are in darkness, grant us to know Thy Son,
Jesus Christ, that through Him we may know Thee. Help
us, that we may not stumble at His Cross and passion, but
see in them the glory of the Only-begotten of the Father,
full of grace and truth. Grant that through them His

strength may fill our weakness and His light our darkness;
and help us not to rebel against Thy will; through the
Same Jesus Christ, our Lord. *Amen.*

371—*Lent*

WE thank Thee, our God and Father, that Thou hast
drawn us to Thy Son, Jesus Christ. By the memory
of His Cross sustain us in our trials; comfort us in our
sorrows; and strengthen us against temptation. Grant that
it may be to us a continuing promise of the forgiveness of
our sins and an eternal life of righteousness with Thee:
through the Same Jesus Christ, Thy Son. *Amen.*

372—*Lent—For the Church of Christ*

O OUR LORD, before Thy Cross of agony, suffered that
we might be one in Thee, we mourn the divisions
which separate us, Thy blood-bought brethren, from each
other: Grant us, O our God, to lose ourselves and all that
is petty and unholy in Thee, and to thirst for the accomplishment of Thy will in us and in all who name Thee Lord;
that as Thou hast died for all, so Thy Church in all the
world may be one in Thee. *Amen.*

373—*Lent*

O LOVING LORD, Who hast bid us follow Thee:
Sanctify our hearts and lives to daily fellowship with
Thee, and here let us learn the things of life and eternity;
let us find the meeting place of eternal love and purpose
reaching into the depths of our sin and woe and pain; and
of Thy great compassion translate life for us to the height
of conquest and fulfillment. *Amen.*

374—*Lent—To Learn to Forgive*

O PITYING LORD JESUS, grant us of Thy gentleness
and meekness, of Thy compassion and love, of Thy
great-heartedness, that filled with Thy grace we may always
forgive the wrongs and evils done us, and seek the blessings
of Thy Cross for those who hurt us. *Amen.*

375—*Holy Week—Palm Sunday*

O ETERNAL and Peaceful King of Sion, Who, as Scripture foretold, didst ride into Jerusalem and manifest Thine everlasting spiritual Kingdom; Who hast brought us peace and victory, righteousness and salvation: Keep us in this Kingdom of God on earth, and help us ever to rejoice and comfort ourselves with Thy protection and Presence, serving Thy Kingdom with all that we are and have, valiantly fighting against all Thine enemies with the power of prayer and true teaching, until all who strive against Thee have been put under Thy feet and we enter into Thine eternal Kingdom. *Amen.*

376—*Maundy Thursday—Of the Lord's Supper*

O LORD GOD, Heavenly Father, we give Thee high praise and thanks for Thy grace, in that, through Thy Son, Thou didst ordain this Supper, in which we eat His Body and drink His Blood: we beseech Thee, help us by Thy Holy Spirit not to use this gift unworthily, but to acknowledge and forsake our sins, confidently believe they are forgiven through Christ, and grow in faith and love from day to day, until we come at the last to the joy of eternal salvation; through the Same, Thy Son, Jesus Christ, our Lord. *Amen.*

377—*Good Friday—(Prayer of the Passion of our Lord)*

O LORD JESUS CHRIST, Son of the Living God, Who for our redemption, wast willing to be born,—circumcised,—reprobated by the Jews,—delivered up by Judas' kiss,—taken and bound,—and carried in chains before Annas, Caiaphas, Herod, and Pilate,—mocked before them, —struck in the face,—smitten with scourge and reed,—to have Thy face veiled and spit upon,—crowned with thorns, —accused by false witnesses,—judged,—and as an innocent Lamb, bearing Thy Cross, led forth for sacrifice,— pierced with nails,—given gall and vinegar to drink,—and condemned to the most infamous death on the Cross,—and to be wounded with the lance: Do Thou, by these most sacred expiations, free us from all sins and punishment, and through Thy holy Cross bring us miserable sinners where Thou didst lead the thief, crucified with Thee, on his late repentance, to be with Thyself eternally; Who livest and reignest with the Father and the Holy Ghost, Oue God, world without end. *Amen.*

ON THE SEVEN WORDS OF THE CROSS

378—*The First Word*

O LORD JESUS CHRIST, Prince of Peace, Who, when Thou wast reviled, didst not revile again, and Who on the Cross didst pray for those who nailed Thee there: Implant in our hearts the virtues of gentleness and patience, that we may overcome evil with good, for Thy sake love our enemies, and as children of our heavenly Father seek Thy peace, and evermore rejoice in Thy love. *Amen.*

379—*The Second Word*

O HOLY JESUS, Who, of Thine infinite mercy, didst accept the conversion of a sinner upon the Cross: Open Thine eyes of mercy, we beseech Thee, upon all those who know Thy love yet delay giving Thee their allegiance and devotion; and of Thy pity hasten the day when all men, drawn to Thee by Thy Cross, shall call Thee Lord and Master and rejoice in life dedicated to Thee. *Amen.*

380—*The Third Word*

O LORD JESUS, Who while Thou didst suffer the agony of the Cross didst show Thy love for Thy sorrowing Mother: We implore Thee, regard in tender pity all parents whose hearts are torn by the loss of loved ones or heavily laden with worries over self-willed and strayed children; and, of Thy mercy, gather all within the peace of Thy Cross, so that the bond of parenthood and childhood may be welded in love of Thee. *Amen.*

381—*The Fourth Word*

O GOD, Almighty Creator of heaven and earth, Who holdest in Thine hand all the might of man: Forsake not Thy world which Thy Son hath redeemed by His holy Cross, but which is sore beset by the power of sin and the evils of man; that righteousness may be the health of every nation and the glory of Christ's salvation may be the sure possession of every heart. *Amen.*

382—*The Fifth Word*

O LORD AND SAVIOUR, Who didst endure the Cross for our sakes, and in bitterest suffering of flesh and spirit didst atone for our sins: We thirst for Thy healing strength, and beseech Thee, be present with us in all hours of pain and anguish, ever bringing to our remembrance this all which Thou hast borne for us; and strengthen us to carry our burdens and to endure our sufferings by the grace of Thy holy example, always giving Thee thanks for Thy love. *Amen.*

383—*The Sixth Word*

O LORD JESUS CHRIST, Who art the Author and Finisher of our faith: Bring to fruition in us that good work which Thou didst accomplish for us, so that we may have the triumphant joy of accomplishing our life in Thee; through Thy mercy, O our God, Who art victorious now and evermore. *Amen.*

384—*The Seventh Word*

O LORD JESUS CHRIST, Who ever livest to make intercession for us; Who hast taken the sting from death and robbed the grave of its victory; to Whom is given the Name which is above every name, for Thou art Lord of all: We implore Thee, that, washed of our sin in Thy Blood, and made children of God through Thy victory, and ever strengthened by Thy grace, we may be Thine through all our days and in the hour of our death; so that by Thy mercy we may taste the fruition of Thy glorious triumph and come to the peace and joy which Thou hast prepared for those who love Thee, Who with the Father and the Holy Ghost, livest and reignest, God, blessed now and evermore. *Amen.*

385—*Easter Eve*

O LORD, Wonderfully Risen Christ, have mercy upon us; spare us, we pray, by the glorious virtue of Thy holy passion and resurrection; and as Thou didst restore the thief a citizen of paradise, so through the victory of Thy Cross free all the world from evil and restore Thy universal creation; so that we whom the darkness of evil conscience hath cast down into sorrow, the perfect splendor of Thy resurrection may raise to victory; through Thy mercy, O our God, Who art blessed for evermore. *Amen.*

386—*Easter (Early Morning)*

ALMIGHTY FATHER, Who through the eternal victory of Thy Son, hast brought us through the shadow of the Cross and the gloom of the garden and the night of the tomb to the glorious sunrise of everlasting light and life: Fill us with the glory of His victory so that transformed and strengthened by Him, we may overcome all that separates us from Thee in this life, and through Him come to the life that never ends, where Thou, O Father, livest and reignest with Jesus Christ, Thy Son, in the unity of the Holy Spirit, One God, blessed and adored now and evermore. *Amen.*

387—*Easter*

WE praise Thee, O God; we magnify Thy holy Name; we give thanks unto Thee for Thy great glory and for Thy love showered upon us this holy day: Accept our praises as we celebrate the glorious resurrection of Thy dear Son, and guide us on from this happy festival to eternal gladness, and from this holy solemnity to the light and joy of life eternal; through the victory of Thy Son, Jesus Christ, our Lord. *Amen.*

388—Easter

O LORD GOD ALMIGHTY, Whose blessed Son, our Saviour, Jesus Christ, did on the third day rise triumphant over death: Raise us, we beseech Thee, from the death of sin unto the life of righteousness, that we may seek those things which are above, where He sitteth on Thy right hand in glory; and this we beg for the sake of the Same, Thy Son, Jesus Christ, our Lord. *Amen.*

389—Eastertide

O LORD JESUS CHRIST, Who didst rise victorious from the dead, conquering for us death and the grave and opening to us the gates to everlasting life: Receive, we pray Thee, our adoration and praise for this victory which Thou hast obtained for us, and grant that we may always follow Thee the way, hold fast to Thee the truth, and live now and eternally in Thee the life, Who with the Father and the Holy Ghost, livest and reignest, ever One God, world without end. *Amen.*

390—Eastertide

O LORD JESUS CHRIST, Whose glorious appearing made of doubting Thomas Thy humble confessor: By Thy blessed grace may our hearts be filled with simple and fervent faith, so that every assault of doubt and scoffing unbelief may be defeated by an unwavering and glad confession of Thee, Who art our risen and reigning Lord and God. *Amen.*

391—Eastertide

O LORD GOD, Heavenly Father, Who hast created us for immortality, and through the glorious resurrection of Thy Son dost nourish us unto eternal righteousness; Who hast sanctified us through Thy Spirit: We beseech Thee, bring the dawning of the everlasting Easter Day and take us safely through death and the grave to share in the everlasting inheritance of Thy joy in heaven; through Jesus Christ, our victorious Lord. *Amen.*

392—*Ascension*

O OUR SAVIOUR and Lord, Who, ascending into the heavens, didst deign to manifest Thy splendor to the eyes of Thy gazing disciples, Who didst promise that as Thou didst ascend so Thou wouldst come again to judgment: Help us to celebrate the feast of Thy ascension this day with the devotion of pure hearts; so that we may rise above the things of earth to better and holier living, that when Thou comest to judgment we may behold Thy appearing with gladness of heart; through Thy mercy, O our God, Who art blessed for evermore. *Amen.*

393—*Ascension*

A LMIGHTY GOD, Whose blessed Son, our Saviour, Jesus Christ, ascended far above all heavens that He might fill all things: Mercifully give us faith to perceive that, according to His promise, He abideth with His Church on earth, even unto the end of the world; through the Same Jesus Christ, our Lord. *Amen.*

394—*Whitsunday*

O LORD JESUS CHRIST, Who art faithful in all Thy words, and holy in all Thy works, we know not what to pray for as we ought: Grant, therefore, that Thy Spirit may intercede for us; sanctify us with His gifts here, and crown us with blessedness hereafter; through Thy mercy, O our God, Who art blessed for evermore. *Amen.*

395—*Whitsunday*

O ALMIGHTY GOD, Who on the day of Pentecost didst send the Holy Ghost, the Comforter, to abide in Thy Church unto the end: Bestow upon us and upon all Thy faithful people His manifold gifts of grace, that with minds enlightened by His truth, and hearts purified by His Presence, we may day by day be strengthened with power in the inward man; through Jesus Christ, our Lord. *Amen.*

396—*Whitsuntide (The Holy Spirit)*

GRANT, we implore Thee, O Lord, that according to the promise of Thy Son, our Lord Jesus Christ, the Holy Spirit may unveil to us, more and more richly, **the** secret of Thy love, and graciously reveal to us all truth; through the Same, Jesus Christ, our Lord. *Amen.*

397—*Trinity*

OUR FATHER, Who didst reveal and teach us the way of life in Thy Son Jesus, and through Thy Holy Spirit dost enlighten our hearts and nourish us in this truth: Receive, we humbly pray, our worship and thanksgiving for this Thy grace, and, enriched with the gifts of Thy Spirit, help us ever to adore and call upon Thee, the Father of mercy and love, as we have been taught by Thy Son Jesus Christ, our Lord. *Amen.*

398—*Trinity*

O LORD GOD ALMIGHTY, Eternal, Immortal, Invisible, the mysteries of Whose Being are unsearchable: Accept, we beseech Thee, our praises for the revelation which Thou hast made of Thyself, Father, Son, and Holy Ghost, Three Persons, and One God; and mercifully grant, that ever holding fast this faith, we may magnify Thy glorious Name; Who livest and reignest, God, blessed now and evermore. *Amen.*

399—*The Last Sunday after the Festival of the Holy Trinity*

O GOD, Eternal, Author and Giver of Life, Who didst give us Thy Son Jesus, that in Him we might have the life that knows no ending: Finish our faith in the victory that overcometh the world, that, of Thy grace,—and not of our desert,—we may be with Thee for evermore, and with all the adoring host praise Thee, Father, Son, and Holy Ghost, in the home of life and love and light and peace eternal. *Amen.*

All Saints' Day—See No. 320.

General Prayers

The *General Prayer* appointed in the Service shall always be used on Festivals and whenever there is a Communion. At other times the *Litany* or a selection from the *Collects and Prayers,* or any other suitable Prayer, may be said.

The Common Service Book
General Rubrics

GENERAL PRAYERS

Adoration

O GOD, King eternal, immortal, invisible, the only wise God, all honor and glory be unto Thee.

O God, the Father of Jesus Christ, our Lord, Who hast taught us to know Thee, through Whom we approach Thee, in Whom we love Thee, we bow before Thee, and in humbleness of spirit but with glad confidence we lift up our hearts and adore Thee. Through Him Who is the living way to Thy glorious Presence we come to join the adoring company of all who bend the knee before Thee, and with our voice unite with the hosts of heaven, who unceasingly magnify Thee, saying,

Holy, Holy, Holy, Lord God of Sabaoth, Heaven and earth are full of Thy glory.

All glory and honor be unto Thee, O Blessed God, Father, Son, and Holy Ghost, now and evermore. *Amen.*

Praise and Adoration

BLESSING and honor, and glory and praise be unto Thee, O our God, Who dost ever surround us with Thy loving kindnesses and tender mercies; Who art exalted in Thy unapproachable holiness and majesty, yet art our welcoming Father in Thy great love in Jesus Christ, Thy Son: Attune our hearts to worthy laud by the grace of Thy hallowing Spirit, and accept, we beseech Thee, O Father, the sacrifice of praise and adoration which we now spread before Thee, that as our lips speak Thy Name our spirits may rejoice in Thee and our lives extol Thy glory; through the Same, Jesus Christ, our Lord. *Amen.*

For General Use

I

ALMIGHTY and Everlasting God, Who by Thy holy apostle hast taught us to make prayers and supplications, and to give thanks for all men; we humbly beseech Thee most mercifully to receive these our prayers, which we offer unto Thy divine majesty, beseeching Thee to inspire continually the universal Church, with the spirit of truth, unity, and concord; and grant that all they that do confess Thy holy Name may agree in the truth of Thy holy Word, and live in unity and godly love.

We beseech Thee also to guide the nations in the way of righteousness, and so to direct all rulers and governors that under them Thy people may lead quiet and peaceable lives in all godliness and honesty. Specially we pray Thee to save and defend Thy servants, the President of the United States and Congress, that under them we may be godly and quietly governed. And grant unto all who are in authority that they may truly and impartially minister justice, to the punishment of wickedness and vice, and to the maintenance of Thy true religion and virtue.

Give grace, O heavenly Father, to all pastors that they may by their life and doctrine set forth Thy true and living Word, and rightly and duly administer Thy holy sacraments. And to all Thy people give Thy heavenly grace, and specially to this congregation here present, that, with meek heart and due reverence, they may hear and receive Thy holy Word, truly serving Thee in holiness and righteousness all the days of their life.

We most humbly beseech Thee of Thy goodness, O Lord, to comfort and succour all them, who in this transitory life are in trouble, sorrow, need, sickness, or any other adversity.

And here we give unto Thee most high praise and hearty thanks for the wonderful grace and virtue declared in all Thy saints from the beginning of the world, whose examples and steadfastness in Thy faith and in keeping Thy holy commandments, grant us to follow.

We commend unto Thee, O Lord, all other Thy servants who are departed hence with the sign of faith, and now do rest from their labors; grant unto them, we beseech Thee, Thy mercy and everlasting peace, that we and all they who are of the mystical body of Thy Son may altogether be set on His right hand, and hear His most joyful voice, Come, ye blessed of my Father, inherit the kingdom prepared for you from the foundation of the world.

Grant this, O Father, for Jesus Christ's sake, our only Mediator and Advocate; Who liveth and reigneth with Thee in the unity of the Holy Ghost, One God, world without end. *Amen.*

II

ALMIGHTY and Everlasting God, Who hast given us being, and sustained us all the days that we have lived, Who hast made Thyself known to us, called us by Thy Gospel to hope and peace in Christ Jesus, and brought us together once more for the worship of Thy Name: Accept, we beseech Thee, our unfeigned thanks for these unmerited mercies, and help us by Thy good Spirit to honor and glorify Thee as grateful and obedient children.

If any among us are still in the bondage of sin, may Thy goodness lead them to repentance. If any have wandered from Thee, mercifully restore them, that they perish not in their unfaithfulness. And as Thou hast blessed us in the past, so let Thy mercies be upon us evermore.

Holy Father, keep through Thine own Name all those whom Thou hast chosen in Christ Jesus. Sanctify them through Thy truth, and perfect them in the blessed hope of His coming again, that they may find abundant entrance into His everlasting Kingdom.

Bless the ministrations of Thy servants at home and abroad, that by the power of Thy Word all unbelief, heresy, and superstition may be purged away from Thy Church. Stir up the hearts and minds of Thy people to more vigorous faith, more earnestness of endeavor, more energy of self-consecration, in the upbuilding of Thy Church and the winning of souls from the ways of death. Baptize them afresh with the Holy Ghost and with power, and rekindle the fires of devotion among them, that men may behold Thy glory, and sinners may be converted unto Thee.

Awaken Christian parents to their duty toward the children they have consecrated to Thee in holy Baptism, that the young may be trained up to useful and honest living, and confess and adorn the doctrine of their Lord and Saviour.

Hinder and suppress all bad influences that would undermine the order and peace of society, that no evil spirit may break forth to trample under foot Thy holy institutes. Preserve the nations from sedition and violence. Bestow Thy Spirit upon all in authority, that they may ever maintain justice and order, and defeat and punish wickedness and all evil doing.

Bless all lawful avocations, that the laborer may have his reward, and the poor find bread; and so impress upon the hearts of mankind their dependence upon Thee, that they may seek their salvation where alone it can be found.

Send forth Thy gracious help to all countries, cities, and peoples on which the hand of affliction rests, and overrule their adversities to spiritual and eternal good. Let not Thine anger come upon us as our sins have deserved, nor chasten us in Thy hot displeasure; but pardon our iniquities, heal our souls, and grant us our portion with Thy saints in glory everlasting; through Jesus Christ our Lord. *Amen.*

III

ALMIGHTY and Ever-living God, Who hast sent the Dayspring from on high to enlighten our darkness and guide our feet in the way of life: We thank Thee for the light of Thy blessed Gospel, and that Thou hast opened here a place for its ministration. Help us, we beseech Thee, to profit by these Thy mercies.

Let Thy blessing rest upon this congregation. May every member of it be Thine indeed. Establish it more and more in faith, and in zeal for Thy Name and honor. Give strength to the weak; restore the erring; comfort the sorrowing; and be present to the prayers of all who in any necessity call upon Thee.

Guide and defend Thy Church universal, and fill it with Thy Spirit, that all who profess themselves Christians may, by a pure faith and a godly life, show forth the riches of Thy saving grace.

Remember and bless those whom Thou hast called to minister in holy things. Uphold and strengthen their number, that Thy Word, as becometh it, may have free course and be glorified.

Protect and prosper all just government, all good laws, and all righteous administration, that Thy people may be enabled to serve Thee in quietness and comfort.

Turn the hearts of the enemies of Thy truth, and of all persecutors of Thy people, that they may find mercy, and learn obedience to Thy holy will.

Awaken the careless and indifferent, and bring them to repentance and a better life.

Direct all inquiring souls into the right way, that they may find peace in believing, and joy in the Holy Ghost.

And grant unto us such knowledge of Thy saving truth, that, amid the vicissitudes and trials of this present life, we may surely trust in Jesus, our Saviour, and be kept without fear until we come into Thine everlasting Kingdom; through Jesus Christ our Lord. *Amen.*

IV

O THOU King Eternal and Lord of all, Whose worthy praise no thought of man or power of speech is competent to render: Accept our humble thanks for the creation of the heavenly hosts, for the making of man in Thine image, for the capacity of Thy creatures to share Thy grace and rejoice in Thy glory, and for the sending of Thine

Only-begotten Son to redeem us from condemnation and to give eternal salvation to all who believe. And for His sake, O God, regard not the impurity of our lips, nor the wickedness of our hearts, but send upon us Thy Holy Spirit, Who worketh faith and sanctification, that He may engraft Thy holy Word and sacraments, that we may have good hope of everlasting life, and offer our supplication in sure confidence that Thou wilt not turn us empty away.

Be mindful, O Lord, of Thy holy Church, here and everywhere, and graciously preserve it in grateful obedience to Thy Word, and in all good works.

Be mindful of all ministers of Thy Church. Purge away from them all error, carnal ambition, and unfaithfulness; enlighten and change the hearts of those who have no right knowledge of Thy Gospel; and increase the number of those whose meat and drink it is to gather and feed Thy flock.

Remember all kings, rulers, and magistrates, that through their government and administrations there may be peace on the earth, and all wars, discord and contention reduced to quietness and amity.

As Thou holdest the righteous from the beginning of the world in everlasting remembrance, grant that we may worthily follow their faith and virtues, and by their example and teachings be imbued with that doctrine which is the true bread of life.

Remember all those who do kind offices to Thy Church, and to their fellowmen; who minister to the necessities of saints; who exercise compassion toward the poor and ignorant; and who give of their substance to build up Thy cause and Kingdom. Plentifully reward them, O God, in the day of Thy righteous judgment.

Be Thou the Comforter of the bereaved and sorrowing, the Support of the aged and infirm, the Guide of the young and inexperienced, the Defender of the wronged and oppressed, and the Deliverer of those assailed and tempted by the evil one.

O Thou, Who dispensest needful sustenance to all Thy creatures, be pleased out of Thine abundance to supply what is requisite for our constant wants of body and soul. Especially turn from us the wrath and punishments due to our sins, and so help and direct us in this life, that when Thine Only-begotten Son cometh to gather His saints, no fondness for our passions or burden of our sins may hinder us from being among His elect. And in this, and in all other things, may Thy Name be glorified, world without end. *Amen.*

V

A General Intercession

O GOD, Almighty and Merciful, let Thy Fatherly kindness be upon all whom Thou hast made. Hear the prayers of all that call upon Thee; open the eyes of them that never pray for themselves; pity the plight of such as are in misery; deal mercifully with them that are in darkness; increase the number and graces of such as fear and serve Thee daily. Preserve this land from the misfortunes of war; this Church from all wild and dangerous errors; this people from forgetting Thee their Lord and Benefactor. Be gracious to all those countries that are made desolate by the sword, famine, pestilence, or persecution. Bless all persons and places to which Thy providence has made us debtors; all who have been instrumental to our good by their assistance, advice, example, or writings, and make us in turn useful to others. Let none of those that desire our prayers want Thy mercy, but defend and comfort and conduct them through to their life's end; for the sake of Jesus Christ our Lord. *Amen.*

For Advent

I

ALMIGHTY GOD, Who art the Hope of all the earth: We enter into Thy Presence with adoration and thanksgiving for the advent of Thine Only-begotten Son in the flesh, and we pray Thee to give us grace to receive

Him, our Saviour and King. Enable us by Thy Holy Spirit so to serve Him in this life with all our powers, that we may stand accepted before Him in that day when He shall come again to judge the quick and the dead.

We thank Thee for the advent of Thy divine Kingdom into the world. Grant us the gift of true repentance, that Thy Kingdom may come even unto us, that it may dwell in our hearts, and that we may know its glory and beauty.

We thank Thee for the advent of Thy holy Church among men. Help us ever to be worthy and faithful members of the mystical Body of Thy Son. Bless all to whom Thou hast committed the rule of Thy Church in the world; and grant that they may minister to Thy glory and Thy people's salvation.

We thank Thee for the universal mission of Thy holy Church. Make known to all nations and peoples Thy mercy and loving-kindness in Jesus Christ. Bless the labors of those who proclaim the Gospel of Thy Son. Give us the will and the wisdom to bear constant witness for Him, Who is our Redeemer and Lord.

We thank Thee for the diversities of gifts in Thy holy Church. Make us to know the one spirit, Who alone can animate and make useful the institutions of the Church. Send Thy heavenly benediction upon all colleges and seminaries, and so guide all who teach and learn, that they may not fail to impart and acquire true wisdom. Look upon our homes of refuge, and be present with those who seek their care and protection.

We pray Thee to bless our rulers and magistrates, giving them grace to seek only Thy favor and the welfare of Thy people. Bless our community and nation. Increase every good work, and grant that men may enjoy the fruits of their toil and eat their bread with thanksgiving.

We beseech Thee, Heavenly Father, graciously to receive these our petitions and mark our needs, which we set before Thee. Grant that by the prayers and labors of Thy holy Church the world may know the riches of Thy love in Jesus

Christ our Lord. Increase our faith in Him, the Morning Star of our day, and the Shepherd of our lives; Who liveth and reigneth with Thee in the unity of the Holy Spirit, world without end. *Amen.*

II

ALMIGHTY GOD, Who didst promise by Thy prophets to send redemption to Thy people, we thank Thee for the advent of Thy Son, by Whose visitation in the flesh we have been redeemed and made partakers of everlasting life. And we beseech Thee to give us grace to hail His coming, and, rejoicing in His light, evermore to continue in the fellowship of His people.

Vouchsafe Thy blessing to Thy Church in this and every land. Clothe Thy ministers with salvation and let Thy people shout for joy. Stir up Thy Christendom, O Lord, and incline the hearts of all Thy people to faithful worship and righteousness of life.

We beseech Thee to look with favor upon the President (and Congress) of the United States, the Governor (and Legislature) of this Commonwealth, and all who bear rule over us. Put Thy fear into the hearts of all our journalists and authors and moulders of opinion in our land, and so enable them to discharge their trust as in Thy sight, that justice and godliness and good order may prevail among us.

Hear our prayer this day for all who are in trouble, for the poor and needy, for the sick, the desolate, and the lonely, for the doubtful and such as are ready to despair. Let Thy mercy, O Lord, rest upon them, and arouse Thy Church to a great compassion for all the multitudes of the earth whom affliction hath overtaken and despoiled.

Bless, we beseech Thee, our homes and schools, all parents and their children, all teachers and their pupils, and grant that wisdom, love, and reverence may always remain among us. Save the people from intemperance, from dishonesty, from avarice, from the lusts of the flesh and the pride of life, from all idolatries, and above all from the blasphemy of denying Thee the patient lover of their souls.

Send us forth into the days of the coming week with a faithful and gallant heart to serve Thee in our several callings. Grant us grace to live always as becometh them who bear Thy Name. And to Thee, the Father Who created us, and to Thee, the Son Who redeemed us, and to Thee, the Holy Ghost Who enlightens us, our One Lord and God, be the praise and dominion now and forevermore. *Amen.*

III

ALMIGHTY GOD, Who by the mouth of Thy holy prophets didst proclaim the coming of Thy Son Jesus Christ, the Hope of Israel, and the Redeemer of the world: Help us, we pray Thee, to see in Him our Lord and Saviour, and by a true faith to rejoice in Thy salvation.

O Thou Only-begotten of the Father, full of grace and truth, come into Thy Church, and mercifully revive Thy languishing people, that they may sing Hosanna to the Son of David, and bless Him that cometh in the Name of the Lord. Make this new year of the Church a time of gracious visitation to those who sit in darkness, of recovery to those who have strayed from Thy ways, of repentance and conversion to those at ease in their carelessness and sins, and of renewed consecration to all who name Thy Name.

O Thou Everlasting Son of the Father, Who hast promised to come again to receive unto Thyself all them that look and wait for Thee: help us to repent of all lukewarmness and sin, to cast off the works of darkness, and to put on the armor of light. Give us grace to pass the time of our sojourn on earth in godly fear and blessed hope, having our loins girded and our lamps trimmed and burning, that when Thou comest in glorious majesty to judge the world, we may be accounted worthy to be numbered with Thy saints in glory everlasting; Who, with the Father and the Holy Ghost, livest and reignest, One God, world without end. *Amen.*

For Christmas

I

ALMIGHTY GOD, the Father of our Lord Jesus Christ: With angels and archangels and all the redeemed we glorify Thee, we praise Thee, we give Thee thanks for all Thy blessings; especially do we thank Thee for Thy gift to the world, our dear Lord, Who (*as on this day*) was made flesh, and dwelt among us, full of grace and truth.

We glorify Thee for the message of heavenly peace brought by Thy angelic messengers, and beseech Thee, that Thy Church through its ambassadors may carry the glad tidings into all the world. Bless every ministry and service in Thy Church, that light may be given to them that sit in darkness and in the shadow of death. Help all who bear the Name of Jesus to honor Him Who was conceived by the Holy Ghost, born of the Virgin Mary, and for our sakes made Man.

We magnify Thee, Who didst place the government upon His shoulder and didst teach us to call His Name Wonderful, Counsellor, The Mighty God, The Everlasting Father, The Prince of Peace. Grant that of the increase of His government and peace there shall be no end; and that His Kingdom shall be ordered and established with judgment and with justice even forever. Bring all peoples, we pray Thee, to His obedience, and establish human government upon the principles of truth, righteousness, justice, love and mercy, which He, the King of kings and Lord of lords, came upon earth to proclaim.

We bless Thee Who hast given us the supreme gift in Thy beloved Son, and beseech Thee, in His Name, grant us all other blessings for this life and for that which is to come. Let the light and joy of this holy season enter the homes of the sad, the destitute, the loveless, the forlorn, the sinful; so that the good cheer of the Gospel of triumphant life in Christ may drive out every shadow of despair and heal every human woe.

Almighty Father, we offer our praise and thanksgiving before the manger throne of Thy Holy Child Jesus. To Thee we consecrate our life and love and service, and beseech Thee to consummate the coming of Thy Son in the ingathering of the fruits of His victory for us in all eternity; and to Thee, Father, Son, and Holy Ghost, One God, be all glory and praise now and evermore. *Amen.*

II

GRACIOUS FATHER in Heaven, Who, when the fullness of time had come, didst send forth Thy Son, we rejoice in Thy incarnation, and bless Thee for Thy advent in the humble birth of Jesus Christ our Lord.

Glory and honor be unto Thee that Thou hast manifested Thyself in Mary's Child Who dwelt among us full of grace and truth. Glory and honor be unto Thee that Christ is born, Whom Thou hast given to bring peace on earth and good will to men. And we beseech Thee that as the herald angels sang of glory to the new-born King, so we may exalt His Name together, that, being born in us, our hearts may be filled with faith and hope and charity.

Graciously bestow Thy blessing upon Thy Church throughout the world. Prosper the ministrations of Thy servants everywhere that by the power of Thy Word all unbelief and schism may be done away. Stir up the consecrations of Thy people and so establish them in the goodly heritage of Thy Gospel, that men may behold Thy glory and sinners be converted unto Thee.

Let Thy light shine upon the nations of mankind. Send peace and·concord to all that dwell upon the earth. And may our Lord, the Prince of Peace, have dominion among the peoples of every tongue and tribe, to the end that wars may cease and good will may be established.

Let Thy favor rest upon our President, and all others in authority, and enable them to discharge the duties of their station with wisdom and justice, as those who must give account to Thee.

O Lord, let the light of this Christmastide rest upon our homes, and bless all parents and their children. And grant that every gift we make each other may be the much more precious as we remember the gift unspeakable of the Holy Child, Who was laid in Bethlehem's manger.

Remember the solitary and the lonely, and keep their hearts above despair, and show them ways of friendship and good cheer. Draw nigh to those who are sick, the invalid and the aged, the poor, for whom so little is provided. And do Thou fill Thy people everywhere with thoughts of kindness, and make them generous and unselfish.

O God, Who hast been so charitable toward us all in the nativity, grant us charity and hasten the day when cynicism and selfishness shall be done away, and the lives of men shall be filled with impulses of love and gentleness and peace as of old the skies were filled with messengers of song and beauty.

Hear us, Gracious God, in these our praises and supplications. Grant us all things needful and keep us in Thy favor, for the sake of Jesus Christ, Thy Son, to Whom with Thee, the Father, and Thee, the Holy Ghost, be glory and honor for evermore. *Amen.*

III

ADORATION, praise, and thanksgiving be unto Thee, O Lord God Almighty, that when darkness covered the earth, and gross darkness the people, Thou didst provide a Saviour, able to help, and strong to deliver. Adoration, praise, and thanksgiving be unto Thee, that Thou gavest Thine eternal Son to become incarnate, that through Him light and pardon, power and peace, life and eternal salvation, might come to the fallen and lost children of men. Adoration, praise and thanksgiving be unto Thee, that by the holy nativity of our Lord Jesus Christ, we, who by sin were driven out of the earthly paradise, are begotten again to a new kingdom, and to an endless paradise in heaven.

God of all mercy, let it please Thee to add grace to grace; and as Thou hast given Thy Son to be our Redeemer, pour out upon us Thy Holy Spirit, that with right affections we may commemorate His birth, and with joyful hearts and ardent devotion accept Him as our Lord and Hope. Help us with living faith to receive the testimony Thou hast given concerning Him, that we may rest in Him as our anointed Prophet, Priest and King, find in Him deliverance from the dominion of sin and death, have comfort in all our tribulations and sorrows, and in the end obtain everlasting life.

Grant, we beseech Thee, O Lord, that the good tidings of great joy in which we rejoice this day may be brought to every tribe of Adam's race. Put it in the power of all men to say with devout gladness, Unto us this Child is born. unto us this Son is given. Let all that sit in darkness be visited by this light, that they also may rejoice in the blessed rule of the Prince of Peace. May the sorrowing and unhappy look up to Thy throne this day and find abundant consolation in Him Who came to ransom us from every fear and every foe. Bind up the broken-hearted, and proclaim liberty to them that are bound. Give to them that mourn beauty for ashes, and the garment of praise for the spirit of heaviness. Send the joy of Thy salvation into all penitent and burdened souls, that they may rejoice and give glory to God that Christ Jesus came into the world to save sinners. And so help, defend, and keep us all, through Him that was born at Bethlehem, that when He cometh in glorious majesty to finish our redemption, we may have our perfect consummation and bliss in His eternal Kingdom; through the Same Jesus Christ, our Lord. *Amen.*

FOR THE NEW YEAR

O GOD, our Heavenly Father, Who hast been our Dwellingplace in all generations, and Who art from everlasting to everlasting the Same in wisdom, power, and goodness: We adore and bless Thee as the Author of our being, the Source of all our comforts, and the Giver of every good and perfect gift.

Thy gracious providence hath brought us to this day; and it is of Thy mercy that we have not been consumed. Year after year Thou hast spared and blessed us. Thou hast not dealt with us according to our sins, nor rewarded us according to our iniquities. Our afflictions have been fewer than our offenses, and Thy benefactions have been more than we can number. Thou hast continued unto us Thy Word and the sacred ordinances of Thy house. Thou hast filled our homes and hearts with good. Thou hast preserved us from plague and pestilence, and shielded us in the midst of dangers. Thy mercies have been renewed unto us every morning, and Thy faithfulness every night.

For all this we thank and praise Thy holy Name, and humbly beseech Thee for grace and strength to love Thee more, and serve Thee better. Forgive us, O Lord, wherein we have offended against Thee, and so renew our hearts by Thy Holy Spirit that we may not carry our old sins with us into this new year, unlamented, unforgiven, unforsaken.

Holy Father, Thou hast favored and blest us in the past, let Thy favor and blessing go with us into the future. If Thou sendest prosperity, help us to be grateful for it, and to use it to Thine honor. If Thou sendest adversity, suffer us not to faint in the hour of trial, nor to be rebellious against Thy will and appointment. And in every event of Thy providence, give us firm trust in Thy wisdom and goodness, and be Thou our help and strength, and our portion for ever.

Visit also with the tokens of Thy love all for whom we should pray. Bless Thy Church and the preaching of Thy Word, that this may be a year of prosperity to Zion, and of peace among the nations. Let it be a year of triumph for truth and righteousness throughout all the earth. Let it be a year of deliverance to the oppressed, of consolation to the afflicted, and of salvation to the erring and the lost. And to all to whom it shall be the last, let Thy saving mercy be vouchsafed, that they may be found ready for the change, and not fail in meetness for the inheritance of the saints in light.

And unto Thee, Who art able to do exceeding abundantly above all that we can ask or think, be glory and dominion by Christ Jesus, throughout all ages. *Amen.*

For Epiphany

I

ALMIGHTY GOD, Who hast called the nations to Thy light, and kings to the brightness of Thy rising: we thank Thee for the glorious appearing of our Lord Jesus Christ, Who has made known to men Thy power and grace and glory. Grant that we may behold Thee in all His wondrous works, offer Thee pure and holy worship, and bring Thee an acceptable sacrifice of true and joyful service.

We remember before Thee Thy Church in all the world, gathered from all nations and peoples and tongues. We pray for those who serve before Thy altar and proclaim Thy holy Word. Bless their ministry, that through them Thy love may be made manifest to the salvation of many souls. Bless the Christian people, and grant them faith unfeigned, that by Thy grace they may be a clear light to the world and fruitful in all good works. Shine through the missions of Thy Church with the glory of Thy Gospel that the peoples which sit in darkness may behold Thy glory in the face of Jesus Christ, Thy Son.

We remember before Thee this, our nation, and the nations of the world. Send out Thy light and Thy truth, let them lead us, that righteousness and brotherhood and peace may bless us and them. Give grace and good will to all who rule, our President, our Governor, and all who are in authority, that they may administer their offices in Thy fear, to the welfare of all. Give grace and good will to the people, that they may with a ready will reverence law and all rightful authority as of Thee.

We remember before Thee the sick: visit them in mercy;—the sad: grant them Thy abiding comfort;—the heavily laden: give them rest.

We pray for those who rejoice, that they may remember Thee; for all busied with the affairs of this life, that they may not wander from Thee; for all men, that they may come to Thy eternal salvation.

Let the beauty of the Lord, our God, be upon us; and establish Thou the work of our hands upon us; yea, the work of our hands establish Thou it.

And to Thee, the Father, the Son, and the Holy Ghost, One God, be all praise and glory, now and evermore. *Amen.*

II

ALMIGHTY GOD, the Ever-merciful, Who hast revealed Thyself in the incarnation and didst lead the wise men to the manger of Thy Son, we bring Thee the treasures of our hearts, the gold and incense of our praise. We rejoice before Thee in the brightness of His rising Who is the light to lighten the Gentiles and the glory of His people Israel. We beseech Thee to keep alight within us the star of Thy manifestations in Jesus, Thy blessed Son, our Lord. And grant unto us, O Lord, that having seen the splendor of Thy pity in the manger of Thy Son we may become the messengers of His salvation to all mankind.

Gracious God, we pray Thee to look upon all the nations of the earth and let Thy light shine among them. Move the heart of Thy Church to remember and obey the high command to go into all the world and preach the Gospel, until every race and nation shall acknowledge Thee the one God and Father of all, above all, and through all, and in all. Bless the missionaries in other lands who bear the lamp of truth into the dark places of the earth, and prosper them in their labors. And save us all from the sin of hoarding the mercies of Thy redemption.

Manifest Thyself in these days to all the rulers of the earth, and make them wise to do Thy will. Bless the President of this republic and the leaders and legislators of our land and give them all such godly fear and wisdom that amid all the shocks of change Thy Kingdom may not be shaken. And dispose the hearts of all the people to live righteous, sober and godly lives. Remove not the speech of the trusty nor take away the understanding of the aged from us.

Bless and prosper all the institutions of the Church, our hospitals, orphanages, and settlements, our academies, colleges and seminaries, our boards and bureaus, and grant that by these and all the faithful prayers and consecrations of Thy people the manifestation of Thy love may continue.

We beseech Thy mercy for those who are sick. Give them patience in their affliction, and submission to Thy will; and grant that being made whole again they may praise and serve Thee in Thy Church. Be gracious to those who mourn for friends and loved ones, and let Thy Presence shine into their darkness.

Bless the toilers of the world, all who labor with brain and brawn to feed and clothe and shelter the children of humanity, and add more love and beauty to all our lives. Give them a sense of fellowship with Thyself in the work they do and the joyful faith that honest labor, however humble, has Thy blessing and reward.

Give us grace, who are here assembled, to confess the faith in our daily walk and conversation. Help us to witness bravely to the light of Thy revelation. Prosper all good people everywhere, O God, and hinder such as imagine mischief and seek to undermine authority and order in our land. Send us forth into every day, to its toil and its temptation, as those who go to do Thy will in everything and look to find Thee manifest in sundry times and divers manners.

And unto Thee Who art able to keep us from falling and to present us faultless before the Presence of Thy glory with exceeding joy, the only wise God, our Saviour, be glory and majesty, now and for evermore. *Amen.*

For Lent

I

O GOD, our Heavenly Father, Who didst so love the world as to give Thine Only-begotten Son, that whosoever believeth in Him should not perish, but have everlasting life: We give thanks to Thee for His holy life on earth, for His precious sufferings and death, and for His glorious victory over sin and evil; and we beseech Thee to grant us a lively faith in Him and a portion in the life which He has obtained for us.

We pray for the holy Church throughout the world; and especially for the churches united to us in sacred communion and life. We pray for the ministers of Thy Word and sacraments; (for the President of our Synod); and especially for our own pastors and teachers. We pray for the rulers of our state and nation, for our judges and magistrates; beseeching Thee that all these in their several callings may serve truly and faithfully to Thy glory and to the good government of the people; remembering always the strict and solemn account which they must give before the judgment seat of Christ.

We pray for all Christian people, that they may live in Thy faith and fear, in dutiful obedience to Thee and in brotherly charity one to another. We intercede for all who desire, or have need of, our prayers: (the sick, the sorrowing, the forsaken, the despondent and especially for............). We beseech Thee to grant them those spiritual and temporal gifts which will be to their present and eternal welfare.

We pray for ourselves, that, in Thy mercy, these holy days may bring anew to our hearts all that our Lord hath done for us and for our eternal salvation. We mourn our sinfulness and seek Thy forgiveness and grace. Grant that we may ever rejoice in Thy love and find strength for life's way, so that we may faithfully carry whatever our cross, and steadfastly walk the way set before us with thankful joy, and at last taste the peace of our Lord's victory in the rest which He hath prepared for all who love Him.

We praise Thee for all those who have departed this life in the faith of Christ, and pray Thee that we may be made partakers with them in the glorious resurrection unto life everlasting.

All which things we humbly pray in the Name of Him Who humbled Himself, and became obedient unto death, even the death of the Cross, Jesus Christ, our adorable Saviour, Who liveth and reigneth with Thee and the Holy Ghost, ever One God, world without end. *Amen.*

II

O LORD, our God, the Almighty Father, Who art plenteous in mercy toward them that call upon Thee, and Who hast given Thine Only-begotten Son to be wounded for our transgressions and bruised for our iniquities, we give Thee thanks for Thy goodness, so unspeakable, in the Cross and passion of our Saviour. We bless Thy Name that Thou hast made Him Who knew no sin to suffer for our sins that we might be made the righteousness of God through Him. We devoutly praise Thee for Thy great love, and we beseech Thee that as we contemplate the precious offering of Thy Son Jesus upon the altar of the Cross for our redemption we may lament the evil in us and by a lively faith obtain the joy of Thy forgiveness and everlasting life.

Bestow Thy blessing, Almighty God, upon Thy Church, in this and every land. Keep Thy people steadfast in the faith. And bless the ministers, musicians, teachers, layleaders, and all who labor in Thy Name and fill them with the love of Christ and the love of souls. And may our catechumens, being instructed, renew with joy and faithful zeal the covenant of their Baptism.

Speed and prosper Thy mighty Word in foreign lands. Bless the missionaries and native helpers who toil in diverse places throughout the world to build Thy Kingdom of righteousness, peace and joy in the Holy Ghost, and give them all good courage and good success.

Hear our prayers for students and faculties in all schools of learning, make them wise as well in spiritual as in temporal things. Fill the hearts of our young men and women with reverence and godly fear and the love of truth.

Look, O Lord, with favor upon the President (and Congress) of the United States, the Governor (and the Legislature) of this Commonwealth, and all the men and women who stand before us in places of public trust. Make them faithful stewards of this their power. Grant us as a people such intelligence and conscience about our government that those who govern will not dare to do injustice.

We commend to Thy fatherly mercy those who are in pain and sickness and the peril of death; give them grace to suffer patiently. Bless those who watch beside their beds, all physicians and nurses, enabling them to care for sufferers in the spirit of Him Who through suffering was made perfect. O Lord, bind up the brokenhearted with the consolations of Thy Cross.

We beseech Thee, gracious God, to give to all men the mind of Christ. Pour out upon us all the spirit of obedience and love. Take away all selfishness and impatience, all hatreds and revenges, and make us humble in the memory of the Cross. Keep us from growing cynical and bitter, and if anyone has wronged us remind us of those who have enriched and blessed us, and let the gentleness of our Lord be upon us. Rule Thou among the peoples of the earth and give Thine own faithful people unfailing zeal to the end that Thy Kingdom may increase and Thy righteous will be done.

Vouchsafe unto us, O God, these and whatsoever other things we ought to ask of Thee, for the sake of the passion of Jesus Christ, our Lord, Who liveth and reigneth with Thee and the Holy Ghost, ever One God, world without end. *Amen.*

For Easter and the Eastertide

I

ALMIGHTY and Eternal God, Who hast made glad the whole world by the glorious resurrection of Thy Son Jesus Christ from the dead: We give thanks to Thee for His triumphant victory over death and the grave, and for the life and immortality which He has brought to light; and we pray, that as we have been buried with Him by Baptism into His death, even so we may rise with Him to newness of life.

We thank Thee for the new life which Thou hast brought to the world in Thy Church, that wonderful and sacred mystery. We praise Thee for Thy holy Word, and for the sacraments and ordinances of Thy Church. We pray Thee to regard favorably the assemblies of believers scattered among the nations: bless those who feed the flock, and all committed to their charge. Make fruitful the preaching of the Gospel. Bless the missions. Sanctify those who come to holy Baptism. Make known to all men the glory and power of Thy divine grace in Jesus Christ, our Lord and Redeemer.

Fill our homes with the resurrection life and joy. Let the rays from the Sun of Righteousness reach into every dark place in life that the world may come to know His brightness and glory, and find in the fruits of His victory life abundant.

Make all governments the guardians of peace. Inspire them to seek victory only over the enemies of life and righteousness. Endow all who rule with the spirit of service and with devotion to trust, and our people with a patriotism that ever seeketh the highest good of all.

By the grace of Thy Spirit, O Holy Father, reveal the risen Lord Himself as the Shepherd of souls to the sick and sorrowing; as the Consoler of the faithful to the lonely and forsaken; and as their Staff and Stay to those who this day pass through the valley of the shadow of death,

We praise Thy beloved Name for the blessings of this holy season, and beseech Thee to keep constant in us the lively hope of the resurrection to eternal life, through our risen Lord and Saviour, Jesus Christ, Who liveth and reigneth with Thee in the unity of the Holy Ghost, One God, world without end. *Amen.*

II

GLORY and honor be unto Thee, Lord God Almighty, our Father, that Thou hast brought life and immortality to light, in the resurrection of Jesus, our Saviour, from the dead. We rejoice before Thee that Thou hast opened the gates of heaven to all believers by Him Who was delivered for our offenses and raised again for our justification. O Thou Who doest wonders, lift up our hearts with praise and enlighten the eyes of our understanding, that we may know what is the hope of our calling in Christ Jesus, and with our whole heart rejoice in the blessings of His salvation.

Send out Thy light to all the earth and speed the tidings of the risen Lord. Give unto Him the heathen for His inheritance and the uttermost parts of the earth for His possession. Establish Thou the rule of Jesus from the rising to the setting sun, that all darkness may be done away and every tongue confess that He is Lord to the glory of God the Father.

Quicken Thy Church on earth with the power of the endless life. Stir up Thy people with a lively hope and fill their hearts with resurrection joy. Mercifully take away from all Thy people the fear of death. And if any mourn, remembering loved ones who have passed the bounds of this present time, help them to look up in the light of Easter's tidings, to the land of immortality, where love is ever lord of life and tears are dried and death itself is dead.

O Lord, we pray that the blessings of this victorious Christian faith may rest upon our homes, upon all parents and their children, upon all teachers and their pupils to the end that they may live as in Thy sight, with reverence, and valor, and faithful zeal,

Bestow Thy blessing upon the rulers of the earth and the governments. Especially do we entreat Thee to bless the President (and Congress) of the United States, the Governor (and Legislature) of this Commonwealth, and all officers of the public life, and grant them wisdom for their tasks and an unselfish zeal for good order, justice, and sobriety in our land.

O Lord, remember in Thy mercy the sick, the sorrowing, the heavy laden and save them out of their distresses. Reveal Thyself to the desolate and despairing, and put courage in their hearts. May the song of victory sound again among the fearful and the faint of heart to bring them back, out of their defeat and questioning, unto the glorious certitudes of faith in Him Who was dead but is alive for evermore.

Now the God of Peace, Who brought again from the dead our Lord Jesus, that great Shepherd of the sheep, through the Blood of the everlasting covenant, make us perfect in every good work to do His will, working in us that which is wellpleasing in His sight, through Jesus Christ; to Whom be glory for ever and ever. *Amen.*

III

HOLY, Holy, Holy, Lord God Almighty, Who wast and art, and art to come: Glory, and honor, and thanks be unto Thee, for Thou art God, glorious in holiness, fearful in praises, doing wonders.

Glory, and honor, and thanks be unto Thee, for this the day which Thou hast made, that we might rejoice and be glad in it.

Glory, and honor, and thanks be unto Thee, for the gift of Thy beloved Son Jesus Christ, to be manifest in the flesh, to take away sin by the willing sacrifice of Himself upon the Cross, to bring life and immortality to light, and to open the Kingdom of heaven to all believers.

Glory, and honor, and thanks be unto Thee, Who art so wonderful in counsel and so excellent in working, that He

Who was delivered for our offences was raised again for our justification.

Forgive, we beseech Thee, the errors and sins by which we have made ourselves unworthy of such unspeakable condescension and mercy; and graciously enlighten the eyes of our understanding, and help our infirmities, that we may know what is the hope of our calling in Christ Jesus, and with our whole heart rejoice in His glorious Gospel.

As Thou hast brought again from the dead our Lord Jesus, that great Shepherd of the sheep, quicken Thou us together with Him, that, according to Thine abundant mercy, begotten again unto a lively hope by the resurrection of Jesus Christ from the dead, we may walk in newness of life, purify ourselves as He is pure, and, amid the temptations and adversities of this present time, be steadfast, immovable, always abounding in the work of the Lord.

O God, Who by Thy mighty power didst overthrow the powers of darkness, through the death and resurrection of the Captain of our salvation: Be pleased to give unto Him the heathen for His inheritance, and the uttermost parts of the earth for His possession. Put all His enemies under His feet, and establish His blessed rule from the rising to the setting of the sun, that all ungodliness, wickedness, and every evil may be done away, and all tongues confess that Jesus Christ is Lord, to the glory of God the Father.

Send forth, O Lord, the comfort and peace of Thy Gospel to all the sorrowing and needy,—to all that are oppressed by lawless might, to all who are suffering for the truth's sake, to all the benighted and sin-burdened, to all beset with sore temptations, to all who are sinking under the weight of disease, to all who are tormented with the fear of death, and to all who are ready to despair of Thy mercy; and let the joy of Christ's victory over death and hell enter and dwell in the hearts of all believers.

And now that Christ is risen from the dead, and become the Firstfruits of them that slept, may we ever joyfully

anticipate our gathering together unto Him, knowing that
He is able to save them to the uttermost that come unto
God by Him, seeing He ever liveth to make intercession
for them.

Now unto Him that is able to keep us from falling, and
to present us faultless before the presence of His glory
with exceeding joy, to the only wise God our Saviour, be
glory and majesty, dominion and power, both now and
for ever. *Amen.*

For Ascension Day

ALMIGHTY GOD, the Father of our Lord Jesus Christ:
We adore and praise Thee for all Thy greatness and
glory, and for all Thy works of love and mercy toward the
children of men. We thank Thee for the gift of Thine only
Son to be our Redeemer and to save us from sin and death.
We thank Thee for His triumphant ascension into heaven,
far above all principalities and powers and every name that
is named. We thank Thee that Thou hast gloriously crowned
Him for His obedience unto death, and hast raised Him to
majesty and dominion, as Head over all things to the
Church. We thank Thee for His great victory obtained for
us, and pray Thee for grace to honor and serve Him as the
King of glory and the Saviour of the world.

O Lord Jesus Christ, Thou everlasting Son of the Father,
unto Whom all power in heaven and on earth is given: We
thank and bless Thee that Thou hast blotted out the hand-
writing of ordinances that was against us; that thou hast
taken away the sentence of our condemnation; that Thou
hast redeemed us with Thy precious Blood; that Thou hast
conquered sin, death and the world, that they may have no
more dominion over us.

O Thou great and everlasting High Priest: Grant us a
share in the benefits of Thy merciful mediation, that we
also may enter whither Thou hast gone, through the way
Thou hast consecrated, and have our everlasting abode
with Thee in Thy heavenly Kingdom. Graciously send upon
us Thy Holy Spirit, the Comforter, to lead us into right

knowledge of Thy truth, to strengthen and uphold us in the true confession of Thy Name, and to help our infirmities, that we may do Thy will, obey Thy commandments, and not fail of the rewards of good and faithful servants.

Remember, O Lord, Thy toiling Church, and let Thy heavenly gifts and benediction ever be upon and in it, that Thy cause on earth may never languish. Send forth laborers into Thy harvest, who shall be faithful and wise stewards of Thy household, to give to each his portion in due season. Hasten the gathering together unto Thy Name of Thy chosen ones, and the making up of the number of Thine elect. Comfort the troubled, the faint, and the weak. Set free the captives to sin and unbelief, that they may learn to rejoice in Thy salvation. And help all to seek those things which are above where Thou sittest at the right hand of the Father, and to look and wait for Thy coming again to receive Thy people to Thyself, that they may ever be where Thou art; Who livest and reignest with the Father and the Holy Ghost, One God, world without end. *Amen.*

For Whitsunday

I

ALMIGHTY and Everlasting God, Who hast given the Church Thy Holy Spirit, that He may abide with it for ever: We thank Thee for the inspiration, guidance, and comfort which come from Him; and we pray Thee that He may ever direct and rule our lives, and that daily He may increase in us the knowledge and love of Thyself and of Thy Son, Jesus Christ, our Lord.

Shed forth His manifold gifts of grace upon every estate of men in Thy holy Church. Grant that Thy believing people may receive the spirit of wisdom and understanding, the spirit of counsel and might, the spirit of knowledge and of the fear of the Lord. To our rulers grant the spirit of justice and mercy; and to all our people the spirit of faithfulness and peace.

Let the blessing of Thy Holy Spirit, we pray Thee, be upon the sick and sorrowing, the oppressed and the afflicted. Grant that He may be their Comforter and Helper in every need, and that He may bring their petitions before Thy heavenly throne.

O Thou, Who sendest forth Thy Spirit, and renewest the face of the whole earth, shed abroad in our hearts His love, joy, and peace; that He may recall us from our forgetfulness of Thee and bring us back to Thy heart by the holy way of repentance and faith. Cast us not away from Thy Presence, and take not Thy Holy Spirit from us. Restore unto us the joy of Thy salvation, and uphold us with Thy free Spirit; through Jesus Christ, Thy Son, our Lord, Who liveth and reigneth with Thee in the unity of the Same Spirit, One God, world without end. *Amen.*

II

B LESSED HOLY SPIRIT, proceeding from the Father and the Son, Who [*on this day*] didst descend upon the disciples to give them light and comfort for their witness to the faith, we thank Thee for Thy cleansing and kindling power. We beseech Thee to come into our hearts that we may be purified from our sins and filled with zeal for the glory of the Kingdom of our Saviour Jesus Christ.

O Spirit of truth, make Thy Presence manifest in the Church throughout the world. Increase in us knowledge and understanding of our Lord, the Saviour of mankind, and kindle in Christ's people a passionate desire for what is right and lovely and pure and just. Put within the heart of Thy Church such a mighty faith that the gates of hell prevail not against it.

O God, the Holy Spirit, send peace on earth. Dispose the nations of mankind to live together without suspicion, fear and arrogance. To this end enlighten all rulers upon earth. Especially do we entreat Thee to bless the President (and Congress) of the United States and all men and women who exercise authority among us.

Blessed Comforter, be with those who pass through dark valleys and deep waters. Bind up all broken and wounded hearts and visit them with Thy consolations. Draw nigh to the sick and give them a patient mind and a joyful trust in Thy deliverance. O Lord, raise up the weak and comfort the faint-hearted. Lift up the fallen and save Thy people out of their tribulations and temptations.

Gracious Helper, let Thy light shine upon our homes. Give all parents a sense of duty to their children whom they have consecrated in holy Baptism that the young may grow up in the love and service of Christ Jesus and of His Church. Enlighten all leaders of the people, teach all teachers of our youth, to the end that error and irreverence may be done away and the knowledge of the truth as it is in Jesus may be established.

Holy Spirit, Thou Light Immortal, make our hearts Thy habitation. Teach our lips to make a brave confession. Move Thy people to greater zeal and prayerfulness for Christ's Kingdom. Uphold us in the ways of hardship, lest our hearts grow hard and our courage fail us. Save us from the sin of anger and of envy, from harsh thoughts and unlovely and discourteous manners. Bestow upon us the blessing of reverence and quietness, and faith to hearken to Thy still small voice. Keep us in the sanctuary of Thy peace.

And unto Thee, Blessed Spirit, with the Father and the Son, the Living God, be praise and glory, both now and evermore. *Amen.*

FOR THE FESTIVAL OF THE HOLY TRINITY
AND THE TRINITY SEASON

I

BLESSED art Thou, O Lord God of our fathers, and greatly to be praised, and glorified, and highly exalted for ever. Blessed be the Name of the Father, the Name of the Son, and the Name of the Holy Ghost. Blessed be the One True God, our Creator, Redeemer, and Sanctifier.

We give thanks to Thee, O God, for the revelation of Thyself, Father, Son, and Holy Spirit. Grant that we may ever thank, praise, serve, and obey Thee for Thy creation and divine providence. Keep us ever Thine, so that we may live under Thee in Thy Kingdom, and serve Thee in everlasting righteousness, innocence, and blessedness. Preserve us in union with Thee and Thy whole Church. Grant us the forgiveness of our sins, and the consummation of the hope of the resurrection of the dead and the life of the world to come. Grant that we may ever abide in this faith, to Thy praise and glory, and to our eternal welfare.

Bless, O Lord, Thy Church: her pastors and ministers, and all her people. Grant that all men may know Thee, believe in Thee, and seek to do Thy will. Bless, O Lord, our nation, and every nation, and bring them to the true Christian faith. Bless our rulers and all who are in authority, and grant that they may govern the state with righteousness and true faithfulness.

Bless, we beseech Thee, all sorts and conditions of men in Thy Church. Restore the fallen, forgive the penitent, heal the sick, comfort the sorrowing, and give rest to those who abide in Thee. Unite us all in the confession of Thy holy Name, and in the worship of Thy glory, O Thou, Who livest and reignest, God above all, for ever and ever. *Amen.*

II

O GOD, Thou Author of our being and Fountain of our blessing, Who art from everlasting to everlasting and dwellest in the praises of eternity, we thank Thee for the rays of revelation by which we come to know Thee and for Thy mercy by which we come to love Thee. Thou art the One God, the Ever Blessed, in Whom we live and move and have our being.

We bless Thee, Almighty Father, Who madest all things visible and invisible. Keep us, we beseech Thee, in Thy mighty power and help us to walk before Thee day by day in Thy fatherly protection.

O Mighty Son, Redeemer of the world, we worship Thee. Claim Thy heritage, and draw all men to Thee, and enable all Thy people to do their faithful part to spread the Kingdom of Thy righteousness among the sons of men.

Blessed Holy Spirit, abide with us we pray and turn our darkness into day. Sanctify and preserve the Church and comfort and guide Thy faithful people.

O God, Father, Son, and Holy Spirit, Blessed Trinity, uphold us by Thy mighty power and let Thy favor prosper us and fill our hearts with gladness and content.

We beseech Thee to bless Thy Church throughout the world so that, rejoicing in Thy holy Word and sacraments, Thy people may continue steadfast in the confession of their faith and the loving service of their fellowmen. Give Thy grace, O Lord, to all ministers, missionaries and deaconesses, all officers and lay-readers among Thy people, that the number may be increased of those whose meat and drink it is to love and do Thy will.

Let Thy favor rest upon the President (and Congress) of the United States, the Governor (and Legislature) of this state, and all others who are in position of public trust and leadership. Give health and courage to all just and righteous rulers. Bring to naught the counsels of the wicked, and save the people from violence, greed and fraud.

Have mercy, O Lord, upon those whose hearts are captured by worldly cares and pleasures, who make light of holy things. May those who are afar off be brought near again, and made wise unto their salvation.

Hear our prayer this day for the sick and save those among us who are in fear and tribulation. Prosper those who are engaged in lawful occupations, that the laborer may have his due reward and the poor find bread. May the spirit of charity and justice prevail among employers and their employed so that all of us may prosper also in things spiritual as in things material.

Visit us all, O Mighty God, with Thy plenteous grace. Comfort the sorrowing, strengthen the weak, restore the erring, and if any desire to be remembered in our prayers this day, look upon them in Thy mercy, and grant them according to Thy will the desires of their hearts.

Bestow upon us all things needful, and so direct us in all our doings, that we may serve Thee joyously all our days, and in the end attain everlasting life; through Jesus Christ, our Lord, Who liveth and reigneth with Thee, the Father, and Thee, the Holy Ghost, ever One God, world without end. *Amen.*

III

O LORD GOD of heaven and earth, Who dwellest in light unapproachable, Whose nature is unsearchable, Whose counsels are inscrutable, but Who hast given forth rays of Thy great glory and majesty that Thy rational creatures may worship, adore, and seek after Thee: We thank Thee that Thou hast revealed to us Thy Being and goodness, and caused us to hope to behold Thee hereafter in the endless light and joy of heaven.

We bless Thee, O Father Almighty, and worship Thee as the Creator, Preserver, and Ruler of all things, visible and invisible; and we pray Thee to keep us alway in the true knowledge of Thyself, and of Jesus Christ, Whom Thou hast sent, that our hearts may be set to obey Thy commandments, and that we may walk before Thee in the light and comfort of Thy holy revelation.

We bless Thee, O Thou everlasting Son of the Father, that Thou hast ransomed us by Thy Blood from condemnation and eternal death; and we pray Thee to accept us as Thine own, and to perfect in us the will of the Father, that we may be Thy true and loving subjects, and serve Thee in everlasting righteousness, innocence and blessedness, even as Thou art risen from the dead, and livest and reignest to all eternity.

We bless Thee, O Holy Spirit, proceeding from the Father and the Son, the Illuminator, Comforter, Counsellor and Guide of all souls redeemed by the Blood of Jesus, that Thou hast called us by the Gospel and kindled in us the desire and hope of eternal life; and we pray Thee to continue unto us Thine enlightening and sanctifying power, that we may be preserved, established and comforted in the true faith, even as Thou dost enlighten, sanctify and preserve the whole Church unto Jesus Christ, that it may be a glorious Church, without spot, or wrinkle, or any such thing.

O Lord God, Father, Son, and Holy Ghost, ever Three, and ever One: We bless and worship Thee with our whole heart, mind, soul, and strength, for Thou alone art God, and to Thee all worship pertaineth. Be pleased to accept our adoration and to hear our prayers. As Thou hast planted Thy holy Church in the earth, protect, increase, and perfect it by Thy mighty working, and overrule all things for its good and prosperity. Dwell in it with Thy saving grace, that it may be Thy golden candlestick in the midst of this dark world, and ever hold forth the truth, to the saving of all that believe.

And to Thee, the Father, the Son, and the Holy Ghost, one true and only God, be all worship and dominion, world without end. *Amen.*

For the Festival of the Reformation

I

O ALMIGHTY and Eternal God, Who hast chosen out of the world in all times and places those who have believed in Thee: We give Thee thanks for Thy holy people who served Thee under the Patriarchs and Prophets; we praise Thy holy Name for those who in their generation have believed in Thine Only-begotten Son, His incarnation, passion, and glorious resurrection. To Thee we give most high worship for His saving Gospel, for Thy wonderful grace in Him, and for that holy foundation which is His body, the Church. But especially do we praise Thee (*this day*) for Thy servants, our fathers in Christ, through whom Thou didst restore and recall Thy Church to its first profession in the faith of the Gospel. Blessed art Thou, O Lord, and greatly to be praised, and highly exalted for ever.

Mercifully defend Thy Church, O Lord God, from all enemies of Thy saving Word. Bless the work of the Gospel in all lands. Strengthen and renew Thy Church; enable it effectively to make known to the world the truth of the Gospel; make it, in our time, the bearer of the blessings of light, and love, and peace to the world, that all men may see and know that Thou art God.

And as Thou hast enriched the life of man through the Reformation of the Church, we beseech Thee to preserve its fruits to the blessing of our generation and generations to come. Preserve Thy Word, all good education, our liberties and civil privileges; and maintain ordered government and fair dealing among nations and men. Enrich our manhood and womanhood with high ideals and honorable purposes. Inspire us to maintain the heritage of the faith and liberty which we have received from our forefathers.

And to Thee, Father, Son, and Holy Ghost, One God, be all glory and praise, now and evermore. *Amen.*

II

ALMIGHTY GOD, our Heavenly Father, Who hast not left Thyself without a witness in the ages past and who hast promised to be our help for all the years to come, we glorify Thee in Thy Church, which Thou hast preserved and prospered in all the generations. We thank Thee that Thou hast not suffered the gates of hell to prevail against it. We rejoice this day that when it was brought low Thou didst anoint Thy servants to lift it up. We thank Thee that Thou didst visit our fathers in the faith and show forth Thy salvation in them. We thank Thee that Thou hast restored unto Thy people Thy pure Word and sacraments. We beseech Thee to make us joyful in the heritage of the Gospel, that we and our children and our children's children may rejoice in Thy plenteous redemption.

Keep Thy Church, we pray Thee, in the true knowledge and understanding of Thy Word. Clothe Thy ministers with salvation, and grant that Thy people everywhere may stand fast in the liberty wherewith Thou hast made them free. Defend Thy Church from worldliness and schism. Heal our sad divisions with the spirit of unity and the fellowship of Thy love. Quicken Thy Church today with the zeal of Thy Apostles and Reformers, so that they that are afar off may be brought nigh in the knowledge and obedience of the truth.

Let Thy benediction rest, O Lord, upon our country. Bestow Thy Spirit upon all men and women in public office. Grant that true religion may increase amongst us; and hasten the time when all kindreds of the earth shall come to the saving knowledge of Jesus Christ, Thy Son.

Bless, O God, the institutions of the Church, its schools, orphanages and hospices; its hospitals, its seminaries, missions and motherhouses, and all its boards and agencies; and increase Thy Kingdom in this and foreign lands. Keep our young men and women in Thy power, so that amid the vain ambitions of the world they may not forsake their conscience nor deny Thy Cross.

Remember and reward, O Lord, Thy servants, who do kind offices to Thy Church, who minister to the poor, who give of themselves and of their substance to build up Thy Kingdom on the earth. Show Thyself a very present help in time of trouble to the sick and the bereaved. Draw nigh in comfort to the aged and infirm.

O Thou, Who didst revive Thy Church in the Reformation, revive it again. Stir up the vows and consecration of all Thy children. Give us grace gratefully to remember and worthily to emulate the zeal of those who have gone before us. Make us faithful in our time, in the succession of valiant souls who had Thy fear before their eyes and Thy love within their hearts.

Hear us, Mighty Father, in these our prayers and if we fail in asking, fail not Thou in giving according to our needs. And to Thee, Father, Son and Holy Spirit, be glory now and for evermore. *Amen.*

III

ALMIGHTY GOD, our Heavenly Father: We thank Thee that Thou hast planted Thy Church in the earth, and that Thou hast not suffered the gates of hell to prevail against it.

We thank Thee that when it was brought low Thou didst send and raise it up; and that when the enemy came in like a flood, Thou didst lift up a standard against him.

We thank Thee for Thy mercies to our fathers, and that Thou didst visit them with Thy salvation; that Thou didst show forth in them Thy power and faithfulness; that Thou didst glorify Thy Name through their labors and ministry, and didst restore Thy pure Word and sacraments to Thy perishing flock.

We thank Thee for Thy blessed Gospel, and that forgiveness of sins, free justification, and eternal life, through faith in Christ Jesus, are now preached to us.

We thank Thee for all Thy manifold gifts and graces, especially for Thy merciful provision for the salvation of our souls. And we humbly pray Thee to keep and preserve to us the inestimable treasure of Thy saving mercies, that we, and the generations after us, may ever praise Thee for Thy plenteous redemption through the Blood of Thy Son.

Mercifully keep Thy Church in the true knowledge and understanding of Thy Word. Let Thy Spirit ever dwell in it, to defend it from error, worldliness, and schism. Clothe its ministers with salvation and multiply the number of those who preach Thy Truth in pureness and power. Stir up the vows, and prayers, and activities of Thy people, that they may be true and faithful to their holy calling, and stand fast in the liberty wherewith Thou hast made them free.

O Thou Prince of all the kings of the earth, the only Head and Sovereign of the Church: Visit this land, and all lands, with the refreshing benediction of Thy gracious Presence. Thou Who hast the seven spirits of God, come down upon Thy professed followers with a new baptism from Thy throne, that the faith and devotion of Thine Apostles and Confessors may revive and live again for these our needy times. Thou Who walkest in the midst of the golden candlesticks, and holdest the stars in Thy right hand: Raise up and send Thy chosen ones to cleanse the Temple and fill with holy oil Thine ever-burning lamps. Send forth Thy light and Thy truth, and scatter and destroy the darkness of unbelief, superstition, and falsehood. Break down all barriers and restraints to Thy Word, that it may not be bound, but, run, have free course, and be glorified.

O Thou to Whom all power in heaven and earth is given: Put on the robes of Thy imperial majesty, take up the unlimited sceptre which Thy Almighty Father hath bequeathed Thee, and come, that the whole earth may be speedily filled with Thy glory. Quicken us, O Lord, and all Thy professing people, by the renewing power of the Holy Ghost, that when Thou comest in the glory of Thy majesty, we may be found of Thee as Thy true and faithful servants, and be graciously admitted into the joy of Thy Kingdom; Who livest and reignest with the Father and the Holy Ghost, ever One God, world without end. *Amen.*

For a Day of National Thanksgiving

ALMIGHTY GOD, the Creator and Preserver of all things, visible and invisible; without Whose support we cannot exist, and without Whose favor we cannot be happy: We come before Thee this day to give thanks for the innumerable benefits, both temporal and spiritual, which Thou hast so plentifully bestowed upon us.

We thank Thee, that Thou hast made us but a little lower than the angels, and formed us with capacities to know, love, and rejoice in Thee for ever.

We thank Thee, for the mercies and gifts that have come to us in Thy good providence, and for all those satisfactions and comforts which have sustained and gladdened us in every stage of our pilgrimage.

We thank Thee, for the mission of Thy beloved Son to recover us from condemnation and eternal death; for redemption through His Blood; for the forgiveness of sins; and for the means and hope of eternal life.

We thank Thee, for the country in which Thou hast made it our privilege to live,—a land of brooks and fountains, and valleys, and hills,—a land of wheat, and barley, and vines, and goodly trees,—a land where there is bread without slackness, whose stones are iron, and out of whose hills come brass, and silver, and gold,—a land in which Thou hast set up Thy holy tabernacle and sent forth the light of Thy blessed Gospel, for the salvation of every one that believeth.

We thank Thee, for good laws and equitable government, under which Thy people may live and prosper, and worship and serve Thee according to Thy Word, none daring to molest them or make them afraid.

We thank Thee, that even in our afflictions the hand of Thy goodness hath been with us; that even the strokes of deserved judgment have been directed and attempered with love; that in all our sorrows, sickness, bereavements, misfortunes and sorest trials, Thou hast not left us comfortless, nor blotted us out of Thy book because of our many sins.

Lord, Thou hast done great things for us, for which we owe Thee endless gratitude and love. We have heard with our ears, our fathers have told us, what great works Thou didst in their day, in the times of old; and we humbly pray Thee to continue Thy favors to their children from generation to generation.

Look down with Thy special favor upon these United States. Let them ever remain the home of the free, and an asylum for the persecuted and oppressed. Cause Thy glory to dwell among us; and let mercy and truth, righteousness and peace, be our perpetual inheritance. Enable the President, and all others in authority, to discharge the duties of their stations with wisdom and fidelity, as men responsible to Thee. Counsel our counsellors, and teach our senators wisdom. Let not prudence be hid from the eyes of those who lead and govern. Remove not the speech of the trusty, nor take away the understanding of the aged. Keep the rich from being hard-hearted, unthankful, uncharitable, and from trusting in uncertain riches, and make them rich in good works, ready to communicate, that they may lay up for themselves treasures in heaven. Help the poor, and make them rich in faith, that they may not rebel against Thee. And so support and bless the preaching of Thy pure Word, that all may learn to know Thee, Whom to know is life eternal.

Accept, O God, these our thanksgivings and prayers. Pardon our sins. Help our infirmities. And receive us at last into Thy heavenly Kingdom; through Jesus Christ Thy Son, our Lord, Who liveth and reigneth with Thee and the Holy Ghost, ever One God, world without end. *Amen.*

FOR A DAY OF HUMILIATION

(May be used on Ash Wednesday also)

ALMIGHTY and Eternal God, our Maker and our Judge: Holy art Thou, but we are unholy. Righteous art Thou, but we are unrighteous. Conceived and born in sin, we have erred and strayed from Thy ways like lost sheep. We have broken Thy commandments; we have not hearkened unto Thy Word; we have done despite to the Spirit of grace; we have provoked Thy wrath by our manifold transgressions, and deserve Thine everlasting condemnation. But we cast ourselves at Thy feet, in deep humiliation for our wrongdoing, confessing and bewailing our sins, and earnestly entreating of Thy fatherly goodness to have mercy upon us miserable offenders.

O Lord God, Thou hast ever been merciful to distressed and penitent souls. Our fathers trusted in Thee, and Thou heardest their prayers; they cried unto Thee, and were delivered out of their troubles. Therefore, for Thy mercy's sake, look with compassion upon us. Art Thou not our Father? Hath not Thy dear Son borne our iniquities and carried our sorrows? Is there not forgiveness with Thee, that Thou mayest be feared? For the sake of the bitter sufferings and death of our Mediator and Advocate, Jesus Christ the Righteous, we beseech Thee to have mercy upon us.

Grant us, O Lord, true repentance, that we may live unto Thee, and that our souls may live. We humble ourselves under Thy mighty hand and entreat Thee graciously to turn from us those punishments which we by our sins have deserved, and to grant us grace ever hereafter to serve Thee in holiness and pureness of living. Increase and strengthen our faith, that we may truly trust in Thee at all times as our only Rock and Deliverer. Shine into our hearts by the quickening and renewing light of Thy Spirit, that we may be recovered from the darkness and deadness of these last evil days. Take away from us all indifference toward Thy precious Gospel, and incline us to watchfulness and prayer, that we fall not into the snares of Satan. Mercifully help and bless all who call upon Thy Name, that they may have peace in Thee, and not be overwhelmed by any evils which they feel or fear.

Uphold and prosper Thy Church and all faithful preaching of Thy Word. Bring to naught the wicked designs of ungodly men, and silence the blasphemies of those who revile Thy holy truth. Favor and sustain all righteous government and the just administration of the laws, that peace and prosperity may be our perpetual inheritance. While we remain in this vale of affliction and sorrow, may Thy grace be sufficient for us. May the comfort of the Holy Ghost cheer and support us. And when called to go hence, may Thine angels conduct us to the mansions of rest, to give everlasting thanks and praises to the Triune God, the Father, Son, and Holy Ghost. *Amen.*

INDEXES

INDEXES

SOURCES AND ACKNOWLEDGMENTS

Grateful acknowledgment is here made to authors, publishers and representatives of authors and editors for gracious permission to use material from the books listed below. The reference following the prayer refers to page or number in the book from which it has been quoted.

———————

A Book of Collects—Suter, Pater and Filius
    Morehouse Publishing Co. Milwaukee. (*Used by permission of the Publishers*)
        O Heavenly Father, Who hast filled the world—13

A Century of Collects—Atwell M. Y. Baylay
    Oxford University Press (*Used by permission of the Alcuin Club*)
        O God, by Whose good providence—98

A Free Church Book of Common Prayer
    J. M. Dent and Sons, Ltd. London. (*Used by permission of the Editor*)
        Almighty and Everlasting God, Who by Thy holy—211
        Blessed art Thou Who hast granted—59
        Dismiss us now, O Lord—250
        Grant, O Lord, to all teachers (Thomas à Kempis)—223
        O Almighty God and Heavenly Father, we glorify (*Book of Common Prayer, Ireland*)—179
        O God, before Whose altar—71
        O God, cleanse our hearts—250
        O God, let Thy grace descend—250
        O God, our God and the God (*J. F. Oberlin*)—16
        O God, the Fountain of equity (*Bp. Jeremy Taylor*)—25
        O God, Who art ever present—250
        O God, Who rulest the worlds—235
        O God, Whose goodness is great (*Bp. Jeremy Taylor*)—202
        O God, Whose ways are all mercy (*Leonine*)—206

Acts of Devotion
    The Macmillan Company. New York. (*Used by permission of the Publishers.*)
        O God, Who hast taught us—107

Ancient Collects and Other Prayers—William Bright
    Parker & Co. London
        Jesus Master, do Thou meet us (*Mozarabic*)
        Lord Jesus Christ, our Saviour, Who for man—alt
        O Almighty God, from Whom every good prayer
        O God, by Whom the meek
        O Most Loving Father, Who willest us

Andrews, Bishop Lancelot—Private Devotions
  O Christ, our God, Who hast commanded us

Annus Domini—Christina G. Rossetti
  Parker & Co. London
    O Lord Jesus Christ, by Whom came grace—199
    O Lord Jesus Christ, the First-fruits—241
    O Lord Jesus Christ, Who chastenest—292
    O Lord Jesus Christ, Whose train—113
    O Lord Jesus Christ, with Whom is the fountain—63

Benson, Archbishop Edward White—Prayers, Public and Private
  Isbister. London
    Almighty God and Heavenly Father, Who for our sins—156 alt
    Lord God of our fathers, Who of old time—102 alt
    O Lord Jesus Christ, Who art the eternal Wisdom—103
    O Lord, we beseech Thee to raise up (*F.S.B. No. 62*)

Benson, Louis F.—Christian Song
  Presbyterian Board of Christian Education. Philadelphia. (*Used by permission.*)
    God, our Heavenly Father, Who dost call—90

Book of Common Prayer of the Protestant Episcopal Church in the United States—Revision of 1928
  (Morehouse edition)
    Almighty God, our Heavenly Father, Who declarest—44
    Almighty God, Who alone gavest—584
    Almighty God, Who hast created man—44
    O Father of mercies and God of all comfort—45
    O Lord, our Heavenly Father, Whose blessed Son—43

Book of Common Prayer—Canada
    Almighty God, Who by Thy Son Jesus Christ—117
    O Eternal God, mighty in power—759
    O God, Who art the Shield—760 alt
    O God, Who knowest the needs—121
    O Merciful God, at Whose bidding—742

Book of Common Prayer—England
    Almighty God, with Whom do live the spirits (*1549*)
    O God, the Father of our Lord (*1661*)
    O God, our Heavenly Father, Who by Thy gracious
    O Lord Jesus Christ, Who at Thy first (*Bp. Cosin*)
    We do not presume to come (*1549*)

Book of Common Prayer, Proposed: 1927
    Almighty Father, Who by Thy Son
    Almighty God, Who hast blessed the earth
    O God, the Father of all mankind

Book of Common Prayer—Scotland
  Edition of 1912
    Almighty and Immortal God, Giver of life—59
    Almighty Father, Who art present (*1929*)—68
    Almighty God, of Whose only gift—57
    Almighty God, the Fountain of all wisdom (*1929*)—64
    Almighty God, Who at the baptism—296
    Almighty God, Whose blessed Son—297
    Grant, O Almighty God, that as Thy blessed Son

Church Book for the Use of Evangelical Lutheran Congregations
General Council Publication Board. Philadelphia
(These prayers were written or adapted by Joseph A. Seiss)
Adoration, praise, and thanksgiving—iv
Almighty and Eternal God, our Maker—xxiv
Almighty and Everlasting God, Who hast given—xxxv
Almighty and Everliving God, Who hast sent—xxxviii
Almighty God, our Heavenly Father: We thank—xxvi
Almighty God, the Creator and Preserver—xxviii
Almighty God, the Father of our Lord—xvii
Almighty God, Who by the mouth—i
Holy, Holy, Holy, Lord God Almighty—xv
O God, our Heavenly Father, Who hast been—vi
O Lord God of heaven and earth—xx
O Thou King Eternal—xxxix

Common Service Book of the Lutheran Church
Board of Publication of the United Lutheran Church in America. Phila-
delphia. *(Used by permission)*
Almighty God, Everlasting Father, Who dost refresh *(PZS)*—473
O God, Who dost call all men to Thee *(PZS)*—474

Composite
O God, most High and most Holy *(Composite of Prayers by H.
Stobart and B. Compton)*
O God, Who sparest when we deserve
O God, Whose Fatherly love *(FSB No. 41)*
Quicken, O Lord God, in all the land
We give Thee thanks, Almighty God *(Two Latin Collects)*

Cooper, Charles M. (Written for this book)
O Lord God, Who dost rule in the hearts
O Lord Jesus Christ, Who didst love Thy Mother

Coptic Liturgy of Saint Cyril
O God of love, Who hast given a new commandment

Cotton, Bishop George Edward Lynch
O God, Who hast made of one blood

Dawson, George
Almighty God, the Refuge of all
Almighty God, have mercy upon us

Dearmer, Percy
O God, our Heavenly Father, we beseech

Devotional Services for Public Worship—John Hunter
J. M. Dent & Sons, Ltd. London. *(Used by permission of the Publishers)*
Almighty God, without Whom nothing is strong—72
O God, before Whose face the generations—6
O God, Whose alone is the Kingdom—130 alt
O God, Whose Presence is everywhere—21

Dietrich, Veit—Tr. PZS
O Lord God, Heavenly Father, we give Thee
O Lord God, Heavenly Father, Who hast made
O Lord God, Heavenly Father, Who hast revealed

Hymns and Prayers
>   The Board of Publication of the United Lutheran Church in America.
>   Philadelphia. *(Used by permission)*
>>   Almighty God, Who hast promised—168
>>   Blessed Lord, Who didst condescend—168
>>   O God, our Heavenly Father, we beseech—172
>>   O God, Who art everywhere present—173
>>   O God, Who hast commanded—169
>>   O God, Who hast commanded us—172
>>   O God, Who hast sent Thy Son—170
>>   O Holy and Blessed Spirit—168
>>   O Lord Jesus Christ, Who in the days—169
>>   O Lord, our Saviour—166
>>   O Spirit of God, Who didst move—174
>>   O Thou, Who art the Creator—173

Jacobs, Charles Michael—*(Used by permission)*
>   Grant us, O Lord, an ever-growing
>   Heavenly Father, Who didst send
>   O God, Who didst send
>   O God, Who givest strength
>   O God, Who hast made
>   We thank Thee, our God and Father
>>   See also *Helps on the Road*

Jacobs, Henry Eyster
>   O Lord Jesus Christ, Who didst send forth

Johnson, Samuel
>   Almighty God, our Heavenly Father, without
>   Almighty God, the Giver of all good things
>   Almighty God, Who art the Source of all wisdom

Krouse, Walter R.—*(Written for this book)*
>   Father in Heaven, Who hast endowed
>   Lord Jesus Christ, our Master Teacher
>   Most Gracious God, Heavenly Father, Whom

Laud, Archbishop William
>   Gracious Father, we humbly beseech Thee for Thy

Laufer, Calvin Weiss—*(Used by permission)*
>   O God, Whose Son, our Master
>   Our Father in Heaven, we thank Thee

Leonine Sacramentary
>   O God, Whose ways are all mercy *(FCBCP, 206)*

Lift Up Your Heart—Paul Zeller Strodach
>   Augsburg Publishing House. Minneapolis. *(Used by permission)*
>>   O Loving Lord, Who hast bid us follow Thee—125
>>   O Pitying Lord Jesus, grant us of Thy gentleness—118

Liturgy of Malabar
>   Grant, O Lord, that the ears *(Tr. J. M. Neale)*

Liturgy of Saint James
>   O God, the Father of our Lord *(Tr. J. M. Neale)*
>   We render Thee thanks, O Lord *(Tr. J. M. Neale) (Oremus, 140)*

Scudamore, W. E.
O Lord, Who in Thy righteous zeal—alt

Seiss, Joseph A.—See *Church Book*

Seltzer, George R. (Written for this book)
Almighty and Eternal God, Who hast made
Almighty and Everliving God, Who hast given
Almighty God, the Father of our Lord
Almighty God, Who art the Hope
Almighty God, Who art the true Joy
Almighty God, Who hast called
Blessed art Thou, O Lord God of our fathers
O Almighty and Eternal God, Who hast chosen
O God, our Heavenly Father, Who didst so love
O God, Who in Thy holy Word

Sharpe, G. H.
O Lord Jesus Christ, to Whom the sick

Source uncertain or unknown
Lord, be with those who at this season
Grant, O Lord, that what we have sung
O God, our Heavenly Father, we thank Thee
O Lord Jesus Christ, Prince of Peace
O Lord Jesus Christ, Who hast said
O Lord Jesus Christ, Who in Thy tender love
O Merciful Father, Who hast wonderfully fashioned

Stirewalt, M. L. (Written for this book)
Almighty Father, Who wast well pleased
O God, the Father Almighty, Creator

Strodach, Paul Zeller—(In part written for this book)
Almighty Father, Who hast so formed man
Almighty Father, Who through the eternal victory
Almighty God, Whose blessed Son *(Special Order)*
Blessed Father, in the Name and Spirit
Blessing and honor, and glory *(Preces Fidei)*
Dear Lord, in Whom is all our hope
Dear Lord, our Great Physician
Dear Lord, we thank Thee for our days at school
Dear Lord, Who didst look
Eternal God, Whose almighty power
Grant us, O Father, we beseech Thee *(Special Order)*
Have pity, O Lord God, on all those
Jesus, Master, Who only hast the words
Lord and Master, Who dost accept
O Almighty God, Whose glory the heavens
O Almighty God, Whose years know neither
O Almighty God, our Heavenly Father, Who dost minister
O Almighty God, Whose years know no end
O Everlasting God, Who art the eternal
O God, Almighty Creator *(Preces Fidei)*
O God, at Whose Word chaos
O God, Creator and Upholder
O God, King Eternal, Immortal *(Preces Fidei)*
O God, of Whom and through Whom
O God, of Whose gift
O God, our Father, give us homes
O God, our Father, Who hast established

The Church's Year
> The Macmillan Company. New York. *(Used by permission)*
> > We praise and bless Thy glorious Name

The Family Service Book
> The Board of Publication of the United Lutheran Church in America.
> > Philadelphia. *(Used by permission)*
> > Abide with us, Lord God of Hosts—34
> > Almighty Father, Who by Thy Son *(Book of Com. Pr. Proposed)*
> > > No. 66
> > Almighty God, Who through Thy Son—No. 56
> > Almighty God, Who, when Thou didst *(Oestreich KO)* No. 64
> > Blessed Lord Jesus, Who art ever *(PZS)* No. 70
> > Into Thy hands we commit ourselves—p 17
> > O Almighty, Everlasting God, Who dost call *(PZS)* No. 61b
> > O Almighty Spirit, Comforter *(Anselm)* No. 45
> > O God, before Whose face *(Hunter)* No. 97
> > O God, the Holy Ghost, Who art come *(PZS)* No. 23
> > O God, we beseech Thee to bless—No. 54
> > O God, Who ever governest *(Gelasian)* No. 91
> > O God, Whose Fatherly love—No. 41
> > O Gracious Father, Whose dear Son—*(Armoury of Prayer)* No. 90
> > O Lord God, the Light of the faithful—No. 90
> > O Lord Jesus Christ, grant that the young *(Man. Int. Pr.)* No. 59
> > O Lord Jesus Christ, Who art the eternal *(Man. Int. Pr.)* No 31
> > O Lord Jesus Christ, Who didst yield *(Man. Int. Pr.)* No. 58
> > O Lord, we beseech Thee to raise up *(Archbp. Benson)* No. 62
> > O Lord, without Whom our labor *(Intercessions)* No. 29
> > Our Father, we thank Thee that Thou *(Man. Int. Pr.)* No. 32
> > We do not presume to come *(I Edward VI)* No. 11
> > We give thanks unto Thee, Heavenly Father—No. 25

The Order of Divine Service for Public Worship—W. E. Orchard
> Oxford University Press. London. *(Used by permission)*
> > Answer us when we call *(The Psalter)* 169
> > Bless, we beseech Thee, merciful Lord *(Bellars)* 60
> > Father of mercies and God of all comfort—168
> > O Almighty God, the Refuge—168
> > O God, rich in pity—115
> > O God, the Strength of the weak—30

The Parish School Hymnal
> The Board of Publication of the United Lutheran Church in America.
> > Philadelphia. *(Used by permission)* (* = PZS)
> > Almighty Father, by the advent *—No. 1
> > Almighty God, Who hast granted *—No. 37
> > Let Thy blessing be upon us *—No. 6
> > Most Merciful Father, open our hearts *—No. 34
> > O Almighty and Everlasting God, Who hast given *—No. 15
> > O God, our Heavenly Father, Whose guiding star *—No. 4
> > O God, Who art ever the Same *—No. 3
> > O Lord Jesus Christ, Who didst rise *—No. 11
> > O Lord Jesus, Who hast promised *(J. F. Ohl)* No. 46
> > Our Father, of Whose love the angels sang *—No. 2
> > Our Father, Who didst reveal *—No. 13

The People's Missal—E. A. L. Clarke
> A. R. Mowbray and Co. London. *(Used by permission)*
> > O Christ, our God, Who hast commanded *(Bp. Andrews)* 411
> > O Lord, Who didst command—368

O God, from Whom every good *(Rit. Rom.)* *
O God of unchangeable power *(Gelasian)* Tr. Bright
O God, our Heavenly Father, Who art everywhere *(Gelasian)* *
O God, Who allowest us to celebrate *(Sarum)* *
O God, Who dost not permit *(Mis. Rom.)* *
O God, Who ever governest *(Gelasian)* *
O God, Who hast willed *(Mozarabic)* Tr. Neale
O God, Who, through the grace *(Sarum)* *
O God, Who, through the ministry *(Sarum)* *
O God, Who year after year *(Sarum)* *
O God, Whose Spirit multiplies *(Gelasian)* *
O God, Whose ways are all mercy *(Leonine)* Tr. FCBCP
O Jesus, Sun of Righteousness *(Mozarabic)* *
O Lord God Almighty, Who dwellest *(Mozarabic)* *
O Lord God, lead us away *(Mozarabic)* *
O Lord Jesus Christ, Son of the Living God *(Innocent III)* Tr.
 unknown
O Lord Jesus Christ, Who art faithful *(Mozarabic)* *
O Lord Jesus Christ, Who art very God *(Gregorian)* *
O Lord Jesus Christ, Who by Thy incarnation *(Gregorian)* *
O Lord Jesus Christ, Who in Thy *(Mozarabic)* *
O Lord, make us to live *(Mozarabic)* *
O Lord, Wonderfully Risen Christ *(Mozarabic)* *
O Our Lord, to Whom the sick *(St. Augustine)* Tr. unknown
O Our Saviour and Lord *(Mozarabic)* *
Teach us, good Lord, to serve *(Ignatius Loyola)* Tr. unknown
We entreat Thee, O Lord *(Mozarabic)* *
We give Thee thanks, Almighty God *(Two Latin collects)* *

Swedish
 Watch over us, O Lord *(Oremus)*

Van Dyke, Henry—See *Book of Common Worship*
 As the hart panteth after the water brooks
 Increase, O God, the faith
 O God, Who by the example
 O God, Who didst send

Washington, George
 Almighty God: We make our earnest prayer

Wilson, Bishop T.
 O God, Almighty and Merciful, let Thy

INDEX OF RUBRICS

¶ *Reference is to the number of the collect, except in the General Prayers where the page is given*

For Organizations of the Congregation (Parish)
    For Men
        O Lord Jesus Christ, Who hast committed—54
        O Lord Jesus, Who through Thy Apostle—55

    For Women
        Grant us, O Father, we beseech Thee—57
        O Lord Jesus, loved and served by the devoted—56

    For Men and Women
        O Lord God, Who dost rule in the hearts—58

    For Young People
        Almighty God, Whose blessed Son—60
        O Almighty God, Whose years know no end—59

    For Any Organization
        Lord and Master, Who dost accept—61

For Our City
    O God, grant us a vision of our city—302

For Our City or Community
    Grant, Lord, that we may love—303

For Our Enemies
    O Christ, our God, Who hast commanded us—262
    O Lord, Who didst command Thy disciples—263

For Our Native Land
    O God, Who hast ever been gracious—288

For Our People
    O Lord Jesus Christ, Who by Thy Apostle—296

For Parish Schools
    Dear Lord Jesus, bless, we pray Thee—109
    Grant, O Lord, to all teachers—110
    O Lord Jesus Christ, Who art the Eternal Wisdom—108

For Pastors to Students
    O God of youth, and childhood, and of all men—118
    O Lord Jesus, Teacher and Saviour of men—117

For Prisoners
    O God, Who sparest when we deserve—269

For Protection
    O God, our Heavenly Father, our Refuge—195

For Rain
    O God, our Heavenly Father, Who by Thy gracious—338

For Reverence for God's House
    O God, most High and most Holy—74

For Reverence in God's House
    O Lord, Who in Thy righteous zeal—73

Lent
Heavenly Father, Who didst send Thy Son—369
Let Thy blessing be upon us—365
O God, our Father, Who dost graciously hear—368
O God, Who givest strength to the weak—370
O Gracious Father, Whose dearly loved Son—366
O Loving Lord, Who hast bid us follow Thee—373
O Our Lord, before Thy Cross of agony—372
O Pitying Lord Jesus, grant us of Thy gentleness—374
We entreat Thee, O Lord our God—367
We thank Thee, our God and Father—371

Local Government
O Father of the just, do Thou—301

Love to Our Brethren
O God of Love, Who hast given—182

Maundy Thursday
O Lord God, Heavenly Father, we give Thee high praise—376

Medical Men and Nurses
O Lord Jesus Christ, Who hast said—284
O Lord, the Healer of all our diseases—282
O Merciful Father, Who hast wonderfully fashioned—281

Memorial Days
O God, our Heavenly Father, we thank Thee—318
We praise and bless Thy glorious Name—317

Missions—General
Almighty God, Who by Thy Son Jesus Christ didst give—99

Missions—Evangelistic Work
Increase, O God, the faith—91

Morning
O Lord, give Thy blessing, we pray Thee—322
We give thanks unto Thee, Heavenly Father—320
We give Thee thanks, Almighty God—321

National
Almighty God, our Heavenly Father, bless our country—291
Almighty Lord, of Whose righteous will—287
Bless, we beseech Thee, Merciful Lord, our country—286

Neighbors
Our Heavenly Father, Who dost surround—147

New Year
Almighty God, have mercy upon us—358
O God, Who art ever the Same, and—357
O God, Who art ever the Same, grant—356

New Year's Day
O Lord God, Almighty Creator, from Whom cometh—355

On the Seven Words of the Cross
O Lord Jesus Christ, Prince of Peace (First Word)—378
O Holy Jesus, Who, of Thine infinite mercy (Second Word)—379

INDEX OF COLLECTS AND PRAYERS

CB.................... *Church Book*
CHSB............... *The Children's Hymnal and Service Book*
CSB................. *The Common Service Book*
FCBCP............. *A Free Church Book of Common Prayer*
FSB................. *The Family Service Book*
HP.................. *Hymns and Prayers*
KO.................. *Kirchen Ordnung*
PSH................ *The Parish School Hymnal*

Reference is by number of collect in (   ), except in case of General
Prayers where page is noted

Abide with us, Lord God of Hosts (330)
    FSB, 34
Adoration, praise and thanksgiving (p 189)
    CB, iv
Almighty and Eternal God, our Maker (p 215)
    CB, xxiv
Almighty and Eternal God, the Giver (33)
    CMA; JWS—*The Book of Offices for Special Occasions*
Almighty and Eternal God, we beseech Thee to bless (207)
    Prayers in the Presence, 36
Almighty and Eternal God, Who dost call men (53)
    Luther D. Reed
Almighty and Eternal God, Who hast made glad (p 198)
    George R. Seltzer
Almighty and Everlasting God, Who dost govern (50)
    R. M. Benson—*Manual of Intercessory Prayer*, 24, alt.
    FSB, No. 3
Almighty and Everlasting God, Who by Thy holy apostle (p 178)
    FCBCP, 211
Almighty and Everlasting God, Who hast given the Church (p 203)
    George R. Seltzer
Almighty and Everlasting God, Who hast given us (p 179)
    CB, xxxv
Almighty and Everlasting God, Whose Providence (306)
    Luther D. Reed
Almighty and Everlasting God, Whose Word (65)
    Luther D. Reed
Almighty and Everliving God, Who hast sent (p 180)
    CB, xxxviii
Almighty and Immortal God, Giver of life (238)
    Book of Common Prayer, Scotland (1912) 59
Almighty and Most Merciful God, Who hast given Thy Word (199)
    George Adam Smith—*Book of Prayers for Students*, 128
Almighty, Everlasting God, Lord, Heavenly Father (66)
    Johannes Bugenhagen—*Oremus*, 27
Almighty, Everlasting God, Who didst command the blessed
    Apostle (233)
    Missale Romanum

O God, our Heavenly Father, Who by Thy blessed Son (252)
      Book of Common Prayer, Scotland, 66
O God, our Heavenly Father, Who by Thy gracious (338)
      Book of Common Prayer
O God, our Heavenly Father, Who didst manifest (13)
      J. P. G. in *Prayers for the City of God,* 134
O God, our Heavenly Father, Who didst so love (p 195)
      George R. Seltzer
O God, our Heavenly Father, Who dost call (351)
      Louis F. Benson, *Christian Song,* 90
O God, our Heavenly Father, Who hast been our Dwellingplace (p 190)
      CB, vi
O God, our Heavenly Father, Whose guiding star (359)
      PSH, No. 4
O God, our Saviour, Who willest that all men (101)
      Book of Common Prayer, Scotland (1912) 52
O God, rich in pity as in power (244)
      W. E. Orchard, *Divine Service,* 115
O God, the Father Almighty, Creator (143)
      M. L. Stirewalt
O God, the Father Almighty, Maker (221)
      Luther D. Reed
O God, the Father in heaven, grant Thy mighty (312)
      Emil E. Fischer
O God, the Father of all mankind (212)
      Book of Common Prayer, Proposed, 1927, 124 alt.
O God, the Father of our Lord Jesus Christ, our only Saviour (21)
      Book of Common Prayer, 1661
O God, the Father of our Lord Jesus Christ, Whose Name (179)
      Liturgy of St. James
O God, Thou Author of our being (p 206)
      Jeremy Taylor
O God, the Holy Ghost, Who art come to convict (261)
      FSB, No. 22
O God, the Strength of the weak, the Friend of sinners (270)
      W. E. Orchard, *Divine Service,* 30
O God, Thou Author of our being (206)
      John Henry Harms
O God, to Whom the cherubim and seraphim (35)
      Oremus, 133
O God, we beseech Thee to bless the schools (113)
      FSB, No. 54
O God, Who allowest us to celebrate (363)
      Sarum
O God, Who art ever present (37)
      FCBCP, 250
O God, Who art the Same, and (357)
      PSH, No. 3
O God, Who art ever the Same, grant (356)
      Prayers Ancient and Modern, 1
O God, Who art everywhere present (235)
      HP, 173
O God, Who art our Dwellingplace (141)
      Emil E. Fischer
O God, Who art the Goal of all knowledge (100)
      Book of Prayers for Students, 147 alt.

O Lord, our God, we thank Thee for all Thy mercies (193)
    John Henry Harms
O Lord, our God, Who by Thine own Presence (29)
    Ordinal of the Eastern Church—*Oremus*, 73
O Lord, our Heavenly Father, Whose blessed Son (183)
    Book of Common Prayer, U. S., Revision of 1928
O Lord, our Saviour Jesus Christ, Who in the days (30)
    HP, 166
O Lord, support us all the day long (326)
    Source unknown
O Lord, the Healer of all our diseases (282)
    Sursum Corda, 140
O Lord, we beseech Thee to govern (305)
    Bp. Gore—*Prayers for the City of God*, 187
O Lord, we beseech Thee to raise up (25)
    Archbp. Benson—*FSB*, No. 62
O Lord, Who didst command Thy disciples (263)
    The People's Missal, 368
O Lord, Who didst pray amidst the shadows (192)
    John Henry Harms
O Lord, Who hast promised a blessing (175)
    Paul Zeller Strodach
O Lord, Who in Thy righteous zeal (73)
    W. E. Scudamore, *alt.*
O Lord, Whose favor is life (176)
    Book of Common Worship (Presbyterian) 200
O Lord, without Whom our labor is but lost (31)
    FSB, No. 29
O Lord, wonderfully Risen Christ (385)
    Mozarabic
O Loving Lord, Who hast bid us follow Thee (373)
    Lift Up Your Heart
O Merciful Father, we render Thee thanks (83)
    Paul Zeller Strodach
O Merciful Father, Who hast wonderfully fashioned (281)
    Source uncertain
O Merciful God, at Whose bidding (340)
    Book of Common Prayer, Canada, 742
O Most Loving Father, Who willest us to give (191)
    William Bright
O Our Father, be with the nurses (285)
    Paul Zeller Strodach
O Our Father, Who, through Thy dear Son, dost bid (332)
    Paul Zeller Strodach
O Our Father, Whose dear Son, for the joy (186)
    British Weekly alt.
O Our Father, Whose Son, our Lord (133)
    Paul Zeller Strodach
O Our Father, Whose Son while in the flesh (226)
    Paul Zeller Strodach
O Our Lord, before Thy Cross of agony (372)
    Paul Zeller Strodach
O Our Lord, to Whom the sick, and distressed (274)
    St. Augustine
O Our Saviour and Lord, Who, ascending (392)
    Mozarabic